The Unitarian Universalist Pocket Guide

Edited by Susan Frederick-Gray

Sixth Edition

Skinner House Books
Boston

Copyright © 2019 by the Unitarian Universalist Association. All rights reserved. Published by Skinner House Books, an imprint of the Unitarian Universalist Association, a liberal religious organization with more than 1,000 congregations in the U.S. and Canada, 24 Farnsworth St., Boston, MA 02210-1409.
www.skinnerhouse.org

Foreword copyright © Melissa Harris-Perry, 2012.

Printed in the United States

Cover and text design by Suzanne Morgan.
Cover image, "Aura Chalice" fabric tapestry by Peg Green, peacepeg.com.
Our Work for Social Justice photo © 2015 Christopher L. Walton/UUA.
Our Religious Education photo © 2016 Susan Lawrence/UUA.
All other photos © Nancy Pierce/UUA.

print ISBN: 978-1-55896-826-4 / ebook ISBN: 978-1-55896-829-5
6 5 4 3   / 27 26 25 24 23

Library of Congress Cataloging-in-Publication Data

Names: Frederick-Gray, Susan, 1975- editor.
Title: The Unitarian Universalist pocket guide / edited by Rev. Susan
   Frederick-Gray.
Description: Sixth edition. | Boston : Skinner House Books, [2019] |
Includes
   bibliographical references.
Identifiers: LCCN 2018052452| ISBN 9781558968264 (pbk.) | ISBN
9781558968295 (ebk.)
Subjects: LCSH: Unitarian Universalist Association.
Classification: LCC BX9841.3 .U55 2019 | DDC 289.1/32—dc23 LC
record available at https://lccn.loc.gov/2018052452

We are grateful for permission from Thandeka (revthandeka.org/love-beyond-belief), Susan Manker-Seale, Leslie Takahashi, Rebecca Ann Parker, Natalie Maxwell Fenimore, Barbara Pescan, and Matt Meyer for permission to reprint their readings; Carolyn McDade, Lynn Adair Ungar, Philip A. Porter, Peter Mayer, and Sarah Dan Jones for permission to reprint their songs; and Roberta Finkelstein, Aneesa Shaikh, Jake Morrill, and Megan Dowdell for permission to reprint their stories, originally published in *Testimony: The Transformative Power of Unitarian Universalism*.

Contents

Songs

TO LEARN MORE about Unitarian Universalism or to locate a congregation near you, please visit the Unitarian Universalist Association at uua.org. We welcome you to join us as we strive to work and worship together with respect, openness, and understanding. You can also follow the Unitarian Universalist Association on Facebook and Twitter.

Unitarian Universalist Association
24 Farnsworth Street
Boston, MA 02210-1409
(617) 742–2100
www.uua.org

The largest Unitarian Universalist congregation is the Church of the Larger Fellowship (clfuu.org), which provides a ministry for isolated individuals, small groups, and those unable to attend a Unitarian Universalist congregation in person. Members live all over the world and interact with the Boston-based church staff by mail, phone, email, and social media.

Church of the Larger Fellowship
24 Farnsworth Street
Boston, MA 02210-1409
(617) 948–6166
www.clfuu.org

Unitarian Universalist Principles

We, the member congregations of the Unitarian Universalist Association, covenant to affirm and promote:

The inherent worth and dignity of every person;

Justice, equity, and compassion in human relations;

Acceptance of one another and encouragement to spiritual growth in our congregations;

A free and responsible search for truth and meaning;

The right of conscience and the use of the democratic process within our congregations and in society at large;

The goal of world community with peace, liberty, and justice for all;

Respect for the interdependent web of all existence of which we are a part.

Sources of Our Faith

The living tradition we share draws from many sources:

Direct experience of that transcending mystery and wonder, affirmed in all cultures, which moves us to a renewal of the spirit and an openness to the forces which create and uphold life;

Words and deeds of prophetic people which challenge us to confront powers and structures of evil with justice, compassion, and the transforming power of love;

Wisdom from the world's religions which inspires us in our ethical and spiritual life;

Jewish and Christian teachings which call us to respond to God's love by loving our neighbors as ourselves;

Humanist teachings which counsel us to heed the guidance of reason and the results of science, and warn us against idolatries of the mind and spirit;

Spiritual teachings of earth-centered traditions which celebrate the sacred circle of life and instruct us to live in harmony with the rhythms of nature.

Foreword

Melissa Harris-Perry

You hold in your hand a slim volume with a big goal. This is an introduction to the faith community in which I have spent my life. These are the words of the ordained and lay-people, the certain and the seeking, the lifers and the new-comers, the beloved and the brokenhearted, the insiders and the rejected, all of whom have found a home in the extraordinary, yet intimate, communities of Unitarian Universalism. Do not expect a clearly marked road map. This book does not dictate dogma because Unitarian Universalism is not attached to particular beliefs; rather it is committed to specific work—striking a balance between openness to differing viewpoints on one hand and fierce advocacy of shared ethical claims on the other. This pocket guide hints at our rich, complex, imperfect, and collective struggles to balance these goals while building diverse and supportive communities.

Unitarian Universalists have no set creed, but we do affirm seven shared Principles (see the beginning of this book). If you join in fellowship with Unitarian Universalism, you can hold any opinion you want about the existence of a god and what to call that god. You can change your opinion over time. You can follow your conscience, your readings, your thoughts, and your desires on issues like the existence of an afterlife, the idea of sin, the value of prayer, or the authority of religious texts. Among our congregations, you will find many different worship styles: raucous and religious, contemplative and nature-based, intellectual and secular. You can pray or not, sing in the choir or mumble the hymns, rush out after service or help brew the coffee, collect the canned goods or organize the field trip, pass out a petition or let the petition pass you by, dress casually for services or don your finest attire. Having set aside divisive doctrinal battles we seek a straightforward commitment to the fluid, open, collective work of seeking our truths together without assuming that we will all share the same truth.

Sound easy? It is not. But it is deeply rewarding. The seven Principles are simple to state but challenging to implement. Building a truly expansive intellectual, ethical, and cultural community is not for the faint of heart. In this way, the dogma of Unitarian Universalism is procedural rather than theological. We are committed to being together and to being together in ways that respect our Principles. Our worship and our work exist in finding practical and nurturing ways to govern ourselves and our congregations by living out our commitment to openness, democratic process, human equality, social justice, and personal exploration without harsh judgment.

This little pocket guide suggests some of the reasons we keep going even when the work is hard and the outcomes are uncertain. In other words, this is a book about our faith. Our faith as Unitarian Universalists is not a specific claim about a particular god. It is not found in a single book. It does not rely on claims of our inherent specialness as individuals or as a people. Our faith is messier. Our faith is a belief that we can embrace the common good through how we interact with one another by holding fast to our precepts of inclusion, participation, and nonjudgmental disagreement. Our faith is a practice of intellectual humility, reminding us of our own limitations. Our faith assures us that we are not alone and that we can be part of something greater than ourselves.

If you have never heard of Unitarian Universalism, these pages will teach you something about our history, our faith, our worship, our religious education, and our social justice efforts. If you are new to Unitarian Universalism, these pages will help you learn more about the larger tradition of which your local congregation is part. If you are a lifelong UU, like me, these pages will remind you of our deep roots, our fierce commitments, and our continuing efforts. There is a great deal of information in these pages, but you will not find definitive answers to all your questions. In fact, you may find this book raises more questions than it settles, but that, of course, is at the very heart of Unitarian Universalism.

The journey is the joy. The companions are the comfort. The work is the faith.

Preface

Rev. Susan Frederick-Gray

Welcome to the Unitarian Universalist Pocket Guide! Thank you for the opportunity to share the faith I love with you. Like the other contributors to this book, I am challenged, inspired, sustained, and nurtured by Unitarian Universalism, and excited to offer this guided tour of our values, commitments, and ministries.

The fact that you are here, reading this book, indicates that you have some interest in learning more about Unitarian Universalism. Perhaps you are a spiritual seeker, exploring whether a Unitarian Universalist congregation might provide a spiritual home for you. Perhaps you are a new member of a Unitarian Universalist community, seeking to learn more about these people you have joined yourself with. Perhaps a friend or a family member has told you that they are a Unitarian Universalist and you want to know what that means. Whatever your reasons, I hope this book is a helpful guide.

A key characteristic of Unitarian Universalism is our affirmation of a free and responsible search for truth and meaning. We have no creed, no litmus test for belonging. We encourage everyone to bring their doubts and questions, their evolving system of beliefs and spiritual practices, and the gifts of their own experiences and perspectives. We are life-long learners and all of these enrich our collective spiritual journey. The sources of our inspiration are broad. We draw from scripture and science, from nature and philosophy, from personal experience and ancient tradition. We remain ever open to new revelation that can guide us into deeper engagement with our own spirit and greater understanding of humanity and the world around us.

Ours has never been a monolithic faith. It's one of the reasons we refer to Unitarian Universalism as a "Living Tradition." We are people of all ages, coming from many backgrounds and holding many beliefs. Our faith does not guarantee that everything will be alright if we live by a certain set of rules. Instead, the hope and courage we receive from worship, religious education, community, and social justice efforts call us out of self-centeredness and fear, to a larger commitment beyond ourselves.

These are defining times. The challenges before us, as individuals and as members of local, national, and global communities, are quite literally matters of life and death—especially for black and brown people, immigrants and refugees, LGBTQ folx, people with disabilities, and those deprived of the material resources needed to survive and thrive. Powerful social forces imperil our sense of hope and threaten the bonds of interdependence that bind us all. At its best, Unitarian Universalism teaches us that the humanity of every single person is threatened when we let the dehumanization of any human being go unchallenged.

This is no time for a casual faith or a casual commitment to the values that matter most to you. This is also no time to be alone. Right now, we need nurturing communities that remind us of our connections and responsibilities to one another as a human family. As Unitarian Universalists, we are learning how we better support one another, protect each other and our neighbors, inspire and remind each other of the power of community, practice joy and love, and teach these to our children and next generations.

Unitarian Universalism is at a crucial moment in its history. Like all institutions, we have not always been aware of or willing to grapple with the systems of privilege and oppression in which we are embedded and in which we participate. But that is changing. In ways large and small throughout our denomination, our faith communities are examining our history, our theology, our commitments, and our practices, looking for the ways in which we perpetuate systems of oppression and seeking to disrupt those systems and attitudes that bar our path toward Beloved Community. We are called to put our values, our relationships, and all our spiritual resources to the work of wholeness. Together, imperfectly, we work to build communities and practices of inclusion, care, growth, and love.

I have great faith in the power of this faith to change lives for the better. I speak to you not only as the president of the Unitarian Universalist Association but as a lifelong Unitarian Universalist who knows that this faith saved my life, time and time again. As you'll see in these pages, I'm not alone in that conviction. Unitarian Universalism taught me courage. It taught me to take risks for what is right, to not be afraid to speak up for my values, even if it means being a lone voice. It helped me learn to organize for justice, to love abundantly and boldly, and to trust in the saving power of joy and laughter, of community and song. I am grateful to have been raised from my earliest days to honor the core values of respect and compassion for all. I have been regularly encouraged to wrestle with questions of truth and meaning. And I have received affirmation of my own agency and my ability, indeed the ability of everyone, to make a positive difference.

I hope that whatever has sparked your interest in Unitarian Universalism, whatever your belief or non-belief, wherever you come from, and whatever you carry in your heart, you receive the message of welcome, love, and challenge in these pages. I hope it helps you to embody and practice an unbounded, unconditional, overflowing, and audacious love in your own spiritual journey. Perhaps we can journey together. The path awaits.

"So if someone tells you that they know pain, loneliness, loss, fear, and dismay, but does not know the feeling of being sustained by a love that is wider, deeper, and infinitely vaster than the sorrows, hear these words as a commission. Hear your commission to love, to create community, and to heal. One at a time in personal relationships, ten at a time in covenant groups, hundreds at a time in our congregations, hundreds of thousands at a time in our religious movement, millions at a time as we take our commission deeper and deeper into humanity's heart as a justice-loving people who will transform the world. This is the Good News of our faith."

REV. THANDEKA

Our Faith

Rev. Rosemary Bray McNatt

Come, come, whoever you are.
Wanderer, worshipper, lover of leaving.
It doesn't matter.
Ours is not a caravan of despair.
Come, even if you have broken your vow
a thousand times
Come, yet again, come, come.

Rumi

Unitarian Universalists are especially fond of these words by the Sufi poet and mystic Rumi. His lyrical verse offers a small glimpse of our religious vision—a faith and a world large enough, inclusive enough, for everyone. The fact that we, with our Puritan roots, find meaning in the work of a Sufi poet speaks to our openness to—indeed, our expectation of—finding truth and wisdom in the words of people from cultures and traditions quite different from those in which we might have grown up.

Unitarian Universalism is a non-creedal faith. Rather than a common theology, we are bound by our common history, our affirmation of each person's spiritual quest, and the promises we make to one another about the spiritual values we uphold. Whether you revere God, Goddess, nature, the human spirit, or something holy for which you have no name, you are welcome to join any Unitarian Universalist community and to worship, study, work, and be in relationship with people who are all on their own spiritual paths. If you find over time that your personal credo no longer feels adequate to what you see and experience in the world, your Unitarian Universalist community will companion you through those changes. Your doubts and questions will never jeopardize your belonging. In this faith, which I serve most joyfully, we welcome doubts and questions, and we uphold one another amid all the storms of life.

There have always been people of faith like us: We are the people who sought a religion marked by freedom and reason and acceptance, in addition to faith and hope and love. Our forebears are martyrs who died for religious freedom, ministers who preached that no one is damned to hell or outside the reach of divine love, thinkers who taught us that no spiritual tradition has a monopoly on wisdom, and activists who focused our attention on bettering this world rather than placing our hope in the afterlife. We stand in a grand and glorious stream of faith, always flowing toward freedom, justice, and love of the world.

We are called by our faith to respond to the world, its sorrows as well as its joys. We are often heartbroken about the state of this world but never truly in despair. We who are privileged to be part of this liberal faith have inherited an extraordinary legacy. We have been given the gift of freedom to believe or to doubt; the gift of reason, to consider what we know of life and compare it to the timeless wisdom from other cultures. We have received powerful examples of courage in the service of humanity and of a love that encompasses all life. These are treasures—but they are not ours to keep. They enrich each one of us, but only if we give them away, again and again.

Because of these religious values, Unitarian Universalists have always sparked social change far out of proportion to our actual numbers. We have been instrumental in the abolition of slavery, women's suffrage, the civil rights movement, the movement for LGBTQ rights, and the fight for economic and environmental justice, among other things. By no means are we perfect; we often fail as much as we succeed. Yet even when "we have broken our vows a thousand times," we return to this essential work of justice and liberation for all. We do the work best when we remember what church is and what it is not. Church is not a place to hide. It is not the place to get away from the world. It is not a place where we get to pretend that the lives we live and our particular situations are not terribly complex, often confusing, and sometimes depressing. Church is the place where we stand with one another, look the world in the eye, attempt to see clearly, and gather strength to face what we see with courage and, yes, with joy.

Unitarian Universalism is especially important right now, because something sinister has erupted in our culture and our world again—a harsh and hateful fundamentalism in religion, a bitter, exclusionary, and anti-democratic emphasis in politics. Together, these changes have made a mockery of discourse and a joke of fellowship. We find ourselves living now in a nation that cages undocumented babies and shrinks from the condemnation of violent white supremacists, that threatens the autonomy of women's bodies and the human right to love as we choose to love. Unitarian Universalism, with its deep roots in democracy and in community, provides a corrective saving energy and grace. We understand that we are meant to give substance to the idea of religious freedom; we endeavor to embody it and use that freedom as the fuel for our highest aspirations. We know from experience that nothing takes the place of community and connection, that nothing is a worthy substitute for our ties to the Holy and to one another, across all creedal barriers.

"None of our private worlds is big enough for us
to live a wholesome life in

*We need the wider world of joy and wonder, of
purpose and venture, of toil and tears.*

What are we, any of us, but strangers and
sojourners

forlornly wandering through the nighttime until
we draw together and find the meaning of our
lives in one another,

dissolving our fears in each other's courage, making music together

and lighting torches to guide us through the
dark? We belong together.

Love is what we need. To love and be loved.

*Let our hearts be open; and what we would receive
from others, let us give.*

*For what is given still remains to bless the giver—
when the gift is love.*"

REV. A. POWELL DAVIES

Bringing My Whole Self

Takiyah Amin

I discovered Unitarian Universalism for myself at the age of fourteen, and it felt like something I'd created out of a dream. As a teen from a multifaith family, it was critical for me to be in a community where I could bring the best of what I valued from my Christian and Muslim heritage. I was looking for a faith that could bear the full weight of my beliefs, my doubts, my aspirations, and my questions, without forcing me into a narrow framework of what I was supposed to think or be.

I am a black, working-class, cisgender woman, born and raised in an economically depressed city close to the Canadian border. These things don't speak to the entirety of who I am, but they are huge pieces of my identity and have shaped in many ways how I live, work, dream, build, and move in the world. I am as proud of these indelible marks on my humanity as I am of my personal achievements and professional accomplishments. And when I walk into any space, all of who I am comes with me, full and rich and ready. When I entered Unitarian Universalism, I brought my full self to this living tradition.

Unitarian Universalism, this vibrant and heretical faith, doesn't promise to have all the answers. I have sometimes envied folks in other faith communities who have a neatly tied-up set of dogmas and precepts to align themselves with, even though I know that's not what my soul or my intellect really craves. When we are at our best, Unitarian Universalists are people who will hold you and sustain you while you are living the questions about what you truly believe and how to live that out in the world.

As a living tradition, I am glad to be in a faith community that isn't "closed." While our faith is rooted in centuries-old religious perspectives and practices, new interpretations of what it means to live out this tradition—as people of color, as people on the margins, as people committed to global justice in increasingly complex circumstances—are emerging and being articulated in new and exciting ways. We are a faith that is both deeply rooted and reaching toward the future as we ask ourselves what it means to be UU in the world now, to bring justice now, to be bearers of the heavy weight of democratic consciousness now. The answers, multivalent and diverse, reside in our very lives, so we do well to bring our full selves to bear on this tradition.

What I know is that in Unitarian Universalism, we are better because of who we are together and at our best when we hold the complexity that community provides as a reminder of the holy. It is for these reasons that I do not hold back, hide myself, or shrink as a member of this broadly diverse faith community, and I encourage others to do the same. I don't want any of us to miss out on the beauty that each of us brings to this space. We take it as a given in this tradition that, yes, we are all different in our experiences of the holy, and because of that, we have the blessing of learning from each other as we wrestle with the tension of how to live in full, equitable, and right relationship with each other. This faith has made me better, and I hope that at my best, I have enriched this tradition, too. I believe our faith is made better by everyone who chooses to embrace its challenges and invitations, contradictions and possibilities. This faith is made better by everyone who touches it with their lives.

Saving Our Lives

Rev. Roberta Finkelstein

This church saves lives. It will save your life if you let it. Not just your life, of course, but all of our lives. I know because years ago this church saved my life.

In 1981, I had finally come back to church after a ten-year absence. I was pregnant with our first child, and my husband Barry and I both felt the need to be connected to a community of faith, for all of the same reasons that many people come to church initially: "for the children." But we hadn't gotten involved at all—just came most Sundays and didn't really know anybody. Just before the baby was due, I signed up to join a women's group, thinking that as a new mom I would need some kind of supportive and adult outlet.

And then the unthinkable happened: the baby was stillborn. Devastated doesn't even begin to describe how we felt on that bleak December day when we arrived to attend the memorial service for our son Brian, a service held in a sanctuary all decked out for Christmas. The minister, Kim Beach, was wonderful—present and supportive and eloquent in reminding our gathered friends and family that we had, in one moment, been bereaved and become parents. I will always be grateful for those words.

Also present that day were some people whom I didn't know—members of the women's group that I had not yet attended. They came, they brought food, they introduced themselves to me, assuring me that I was already a member of the group. That group became my lifeline in the following months. They were strangers who became friends, who welcomed me, cried with me, encouraged me, pushed me when I thought about giving up.

My story is a story of pain and loss and gratitude and redemption. The church saved my life. And through this experience I came to understand that the purpose of the church is to save lives.

My story is a story of what happens when we are at our best, not necessarily how we are every minute of every day. But every minute of every day is not a life-saving minute. All I know is that at those times when one of us needs a lifeline, the rest of us are ready to offer it. We may be clumsy, we may miss the mark the first time we throw it. But we will keep trying, and we will gather more people around to help us rather than trying to do it alone. And in the end, we will fulfill our primary function and we will save each other's lives. Over and over again.

The church saved my life. That's how I learned the real reason why the church exists. That's why I'm a minister. Sometimes that gets lost in all the other things that the church does in the meantime, in between life-saving exercises. But all of what we do is in service of readying ourselves for the next life-saving exercise. We have potluck dinners and

Salad Sundays and other chances to get together in fellowship, and we have fun and enjoy each other. The board makes policy decisions and keeps an eye on the budget, the council coordinates the yearly calendar, we plan worship services and adult education programs and musical events, we orient and welcome new members, we teach our children. We do all of these things day in and day out. And then somebody gets sick, or loses their job, or finds themselves mourning the death of a loved one. And then, no matter what we were busy doing, we remember that the purpose of this church is to save each other's lives. And we do just that. Over and over again.

I am eternally grateful to have been the beneficiary of the Unitarian Universalist life-saving operation when I most needed it. In those difficult days my life was saved and the seeds of my ministry were sown. Out of gratitude I intend to remain a faithful part of the Unitarian Universalist life-saving operation for as long as I am able. I hope you will be there as well.

A Search for Truth and Meaning

Aneesa Shaikh

I discovered Unitarian Universalism at around age thirteen, after a long and unsatisfying search for a spiritual community that matched what I felt I needed. I was newly separated from the faith I was born into and had never been more confused about what I believed.

My parents met in college at Baylor University in Texas, my mom a first-generation college student from a very poor Missouri family and my dad a first-generation immigrant who had just arrived in the United States after growing up in India and spending a few years in Nigeria. They were an unlikely match. My mom was raised Southern Baptist and my dad Muslim, further adding to their differences. When they got engaged, my mom converted to Islam so she could marry my dad. My mom had always been a religious woman and found herself quite liking the community that came with the Muslim faith, and once my sister and I were born, it seemed a given that we would be raised as Muslims. And so we were, and I have many a fond memory of Ramadans, Eids, and Jum'ahs from the first thirteen years of my life. I never really had any problems with the principles of the faith or their manifestation in my life, and in fact felt very connected to the five pillars of Islam and was proud of my faith.

But at some point shortly after my maternal grandmother passed away, I started to question whether or not I believed in God, and knew I needed to look within a bit more. I slowly started to accept that the belief in God was so central to Islam that I didn't feel I could continue to practice it anymore. I told my father, who was understandably upset to hear his thirteen-year-old daughter make such a decision. Things were awkward between us for a short while, but at some point he came to me with words I'll never forget: "Aneesa, I realize that in this situation, I can either be angry that my daughter has made a choice I likely won't be able to change, or I can be proud that I've raised a daughter strong enough to think for herself and make her own choices." Both my parents ended up supporting me in this journey, and I am eternally grateful for their willingness to let me search freely and responsibly for truth and meaning.

So began my journey to find something that suited me better. I went with a friend to her synagogue but didn't quite find what I was looking for. I went to different churches with a few other friends but couldn't quite get behind that either. I read about Buddhism, the Baha'i faith, United Methodism, and almost everything in between. But nothing felt right.

One day, while surfing the web in a last ditch effort to find something I felt connected to, I haphazardly Googled "liberal faith community Bellevue, WA," and stumbled upon a blog post that someone had written about Unitarian Universalism. The author of the post was reflecting on their first experience at a Unitarian Universalist congregation, and their description of the community seemed like exactly what I'd been looking for. I found a UU church just a few minutes from my home and decided to check it out the next Sunday. One of my parents dropped me off, and I went in by myself. I was greeted immediately by a somewhat confused-looking member of the congregation who was wondering who I was and why I was there all alone. She asked me what I was looking for, and I said, fully expecting to be met with a weird look, "Well, I'm kind of Muslim, kind of Atheist, and really confused, so . . . I guess I don't really know what I'm looking for." To my complete surprise, she put her arm around me, smiled, led me into the sanctuary, and said, "I think this is just the place for you."

It was, indeed, just the place for me. I kept going back every week after that, and eventually roped my sister into joining me. She liked it, too, so we started going together, and at some point my mom joined us. One Sunday, timidly, my dad joined us as well and found himself enjoying it. Within about a year, the whole family was going, and I think it was a really good thing for us. We still keep Islam very close to our hearts, and it will always be a part of our mixed-up, complex family culture. But we are all very different people, and Unitarian Universalism gave us the freedom we all needed to develop our deeper beliefs and figure out what worked for us as individuals. It significantly changed the way I live my life. It made me more mindful and reflective, taught me to think more inclusively about the big picture, and opened doors to opportunities I may never otherwise have had access to.

One of these was the UUA's Youth and Young Adults of Color Multicultural Leadership School, which taught me invaluable information about cross-cultural leadership and opened my eyes to several new aspects of my own identity. I got to co-lead a workshop at General Assembly in Providence, have given several mini-sermons, and have a huge, incredible network of friends, mentors, and teachers within the UU community. I have also been forced to confront the reality that no institution is exempt from institutionalized systems of oppression. It was disillusioning at first to realize that even within something as seemingly perfect as Unitarian Universalism, white supremacy and other oppressive structures are not only present but prevalent. But this understanding has enabled me to more holistically work toward justice and liberation in all aspects of my life.

I wear a chalice necklace every day to center me and remind myself of what is important. I think often about how different my life would have been had I not discovered Unitarian Universalism, and I always find myself thinking that I would be nowhere near the kind of person I am today if not for the decision to keep searching until I found what felt right. Unitarian Universalism has truly changed my life and continues to do so—it challenges me, frustrates me, teaches me, informs me, calms me, and transforms me in ways I never expected.

The Playground Atheist, Lost and Found

Rev. Jake Morrill

It may be that every elementary school, across the whole South, has at least one self-appointed Playground Atheist. You know the type: When all the other kids are showing off their new WWJD bracelets and mooning about how cool the youth pastor is, there's a sharp-eyed fellow, standing there by the slide, not believing any of it for a second. When the typical debates come up—for instance, whether dogs go to heaven—it's the Playground Atheist who explodes the whole conversation. "Heaven!" he'll say. "Heaven?! What are you, a moron?" Yes, it's this kind of gentle, persuasive approach that has endeared Playground Atheists to junior Christians through the Southland for time immemorial. And, at Bearden Elementary School, as the Reagan years came into full bloom, the Playground Atheist was me.

From time to time, the Tennessee State Legislature will cook up a wild idea. So it happened, when I was in fourth grade, that a reporter from the local NBC affiliate came to visit, with a cameraman in tow. The legislators in Nashville were considering whether to mandate prayer in school, and this reporter was on a mission to find out what the fourth-graders thought.

To start off, she had us all bow our heads, our hands folded on our desks. Then, she opened it up for discussion. Well, what did we think? To absolutely no one's surprise, it was Matthew who spoke first. Everyone in the zip code knew Matthew loved Jesus. Just adored him. Brought him up all the time. So, his eyes shining, Matthew accepted the chance to lay out his convictions. All around the room, heads were nodding. The reporter gave thanks, then asked if there were others. A girl in the back chimed in, to reinforce Matthew's point: this was a world that stood ever in need of more prayer.

Reporters are trained to fish for intrigue, for friction. So, as hands waved in the air, she wondered if anyone had a different opinion. The hands dropped. There was silence. A friend is someone who knows just what lapses in judgment you are prone to make and will leap in to stop you. My lapses tend to involve talking at times when I shouldn't. I recall my good friend Jeff, in those slow-motion seconds, staring at me intently from across the room, shaking his head, and mouthing the word "Don't." But there it was. I had raised my hand. The microphone dangled close. The camera drew near. The room emptied of air.

Later, I recalled having mentioned things I happened to know about the Constitution. I still believe it is possible I uttered the phrase "church and state." But none of these high-minded words and ideals appeared on the local news that evening at 6:00 and 11:00, and again on the early-morning show. No, instead, what the good people of East Tennessee saw was a chubby boy with thick glasses announcing to the whole world that God didn't exist.

As soon as the reporter departed, the whisper of scandal began threading its way through the entire fourth grade. And then the whole school. By the next morning, certain classmates were able to tell me just what their parents thought about a boy who'd say something like that on TV. My parents, I gather, also received some feedback. What I had was not fame. It was outright infamy. Before, my atheism had been an occasional source of wonder to others. They felt the kind of pride you feel when a neighbor happens to own an exotic bird of bright plumage; it was a thrill to be in proximity to something so odd. The Christians even seemed to enjoy my earnest challenges, seeing them perhaps as a kind of a trial. But this time, it seemed, the Playground Atheist had taken it too far. To say something hateful about Jesus at recess was one thing. To broadcast it so everyone could hear it? Unacceptable.

The week dragged on, as I found myself shunned by my classmates. But then, on Thursday afternoon, two handwritten letters arrived, both from the Tennessee Valley Unitarian Universalist Church. One was from my Sunday School teacher; the other from the minister of religious education. Without even opening the envelopes, I knew what to expect. And sure enough, there it was: They were proud. Not of my atheism, per se. But of the character they said they saw in what I'd done. Like the ancient prophets our Sunday School class was studying that year, said one, I had stood my ground and had said what I thought. The next day, the purgatory of exclusion continued. But somehow, I didn't mind it as much—a cold shoulder was nothing beside what Jonah or Amos had faced. And by Monday, it seemed, all was back to normal.

In the years since, my theology has evolved. I have taken Communion, stopped in awe before mountains. I have prayed till tears came and sat in meditation for long hours in a dark Buddhist Zendo. But, truth be told, it was as an atheist that I first came to see, in a way that was real and has not failed me since, how I am part of a love wider than my own life, and how that spacious embrace makes itself known to me, most often, through a community like the one that first told me, "You are not alone."

Not the Last to Need Saving

Rev. Megan Dowdell

When I was eleven years old, I entered a New England Unitarian Universalist church for the first time on my own. I was invited to sing in the youth choir that traveled among several churches downtown. After one session in the religious education program, I wanted to return every week. Arriving without my parents, I quickly became an adopted child of the church. A family would bring me along to the church retreat and make sure I had a ride to come serve food at the silent auction or volunteer in the childcare program. Looking back, I wonder what the members must have thought about this young girl who was always the first to arrive and the last to leave. Of course, what they didn't know then was that my home was not a safe place. I suffered consistent abuse by my father and experienced prolonged periods of silence and neglect. Some might call this *hell*. The weekends, when school was not in session, were the most dangerous times in the week. If there was a task at church I was allowed to do, I would volunteer to be there. If there was any community event or speaker, I would beg to go. My church family truly meant safety and survival at the most vulnerable times.

Just like many fellow victims of trauma and abuse, as a child I believed I had done something to deserve the harm at home. While I remember having dreams of somewhere-else-than-here, I did not imagine a future for myself, or even that my life would extend into adulthood. I do not believe it is an exaggeration to say that I would not have made it through high school without Unitarian Universalism. I am grateful to have stepped into a tradition that rejects the idea of original sin: where we believe that every child is beautiful and every person is worthy of love and nurturing. I was saved by community. I was saved by love. I was saved by faith.

Relationship and trust building are the foundations of my experience of salvation by Unitarian Universalism. At the church, I had many positive adult role models who offered appropriate friendship and opportunities to play, learn, and lead. When I was sixteen and beginning the process of coming out as queer, the adult leaders offered me the opportunity to co-chair the Welcoming Congregation task force. The church confirmed for me in repeated ways what God already knew: not only was I worthy of love, but I had love to give.

When my brother died on Christmas Day in 1999, it was the director of religious education who picked me up and brought me to her house for the holiday dinner. When I was seventeen, my mother went to apply for a restraining order one Sunday morning, so the youth group advisor picked me up and brought me to the Sunday service. The other single mothers in the church became our network of social support.

And it was the minister who convinced me to get "real help" for the stuff I'd be carrying with me from an abusive childhood. "Don't wait until you're thirty and this all creeps up on you." I can still hear her candid voice and see her raised brow, as I sunk into the couch in the minister's study. Now, at thirty-two, I know that I was saved by her respectful challenge in a community that was worthy of my youthful trust, in a loving tradition that values salvation as human wholeness and health for the long haul of this life. She invited me into another part of Unitarian Universalist salvation: a journey away from being consumed by hate or vengeance and toward growth, understanding, and even forgiveness. She didn't ask me to erase or forget traumas that had consumed me but to do the spiritual grief work to forgive myself. Through Unitarian Universalism, I grew into a vision of family and community that condemns violence of all kinds and releases the desire for retribution that would keep me farther from my own flourishing and well-being.

As a Unitarian Universalist, I cannot claim a God who simply damns those who do bad things to hell. Instead I find myself saved in a community that wishes to build a world of justice, mercy, and compassion for all, knowing I am not the last to need saving.

"To worship is to work with dedication and with
skill;
it is to pause from work and listen to a strain of
music.

To worship is to sing with the singing beauty of
the earth;
it is to listen through a storm to the still small
voice within.

Worship is the mystery within us
reaching out to the mystery beyond.

It is an inarticulate silence yearning to speak;
it is the window of the moment
open to the sky of the eternal."

ADAPTED FROM REV. JACOB TRAPP

Our Worship

Rev. Erika Hewitt

We are not at the center of the universe; there is something larger than us—something grander and wiser than our individual selves. What *is* that "something larger"?

Your answer likely depends on your theology: Is that which is larger than us the sum of wisdom that's present when people gather together? Is it a divine force that thrums through the cosmos? Is it God? Is it the collective unconscious? Or is it something altogether beyond our understanding?

While Unitarian Universalists have different ideas about how our individual lives fit into a larger whole, worship is our shared practice of exploring, connecting to, and even *creating* that wholeness. As such, worship is a laboratory for our meaning making. In the words of Rev. Heather Janules, our worship is "defined not by a consensus on theological questions; it is a community paying attention together." By devoting ourselves to encountering and engaging that which is greater, wiser, stronger, and more compassionate than our individual selves, we place ourselves in a crucible for transformation and healing.

If you've arrived in one of our UU congregations from another religious tradition, you might be adjusting to the use of the word *worship* in this way, because beyond our UU communities, it's common to hear *worship* used in a transitive way, pointing to an object of worship (often, a deity).

While there are certainly UUs who believe in God and take delight in worshiping that God, most Unitarian Universalists use the word *worship* in a manner that Rev. David Miller Kohlmeier calls "counterintuitive"—as an intransitive verb. In other words, "We worship" is a full sentence . . . and a powerful one.

What follows is a map through this terrain of UU worship: the roots and traditions that have shaped our Unitarian Universalist life, a primer on common components of UU worship, and a few words of counsel about how to approach our worship services.

Roots

That most UU congregations worship on Sunday morning is the first evidence of its Christian roots: For early Christians, worshiping on Sunday commemorated the resurrection of Jesus (despite our understanding of the sabbath, Sunday was not simply a Christian version of the Jewish Sabbath).

Another hallmark of Christian worship—and more specifically the Protestant tradition that emerged from the Reformation in the 1500s—is the centering of scripture and its interpretation. If the scripture of the Hebrew and Greek testaments was understood by our ancestors to be the word of God, its interpretation was a way for people to understand God and their place in God's world.

Both Unitarianism and Universalism—the twin legacies that gave rise to the present-day helix of Unitarian Universalism—arose from that Christian tradition. Similar threads run through their respective structures of worship (their liturgies), shaping the way we worship today.

The earliest American Unitarian or Universalist prayer book is the Prayer Book of King's Chapel, published in 1785 ("God is the sole object of worship in these prayers," its Preface intones, showing one way our concept of worship has shifted over two centuries). It contains liturgies and prescribed prayers that echo the order of worship in many UU congregations today: sermon-centered, listening-heavy, forward-facing, traditional-hymn-singing services.

Building a New Way

As a living, evolving faith, Unitarian Universalism and its people are continually undergoing transformation of some kind. In recent years, many UU leaders have wondered whether and how our tradition—including its practices in worship—has masked, or even entrenched, systems of oppression.

To counter these tendencies, many religious leaders in our UU congregations are crafting worship using texts and music from beyond the traditional canon: material that represents the lived experience of people of color, people with different gender identities and expressions, and other marginalized peoples whose voices offer us new perspectives and truths to inform our own.

In other words, worship is one way that a congregation (and a people of faith) tells its stories. Drawing those building blocks from increasingly diverse sources results in a worship vessel that's more elastic, inclusive, and effective in helping people create the connections and growth that spark spiritual growth.

The Order of Worship

If I asked you to describe your favorite dessert, you'd probably rhapsodize about its taste or your experience of eating it. You might feel happy while you're talking or even have a sensory memory of taking a bite. What I'm betting, though, is that you wouldn't describe your favorite dessert by listing its ingredients.

That's the conundrum of highlighting some of the components of Unitarian Universalist worship services: The ingredients themselves aren't the point, because worship is a multisensory experience in which something greater is created—a narrative about the people who have gathered, the values that enliven and challenge them, and our understanding of a responsibility to carry that message out into the world.

Another caveat: There's no one way for a worship service to unfold in Unitarian Universalist space. In fact, one of our jokes promises that "if you've seen one UU church, you've seen . . . one." Rev. Wayne Arnason notes that the style, tone, and content of worship in any given UU congregation will depend on its founding history, the scale and style of its worship space, and its musical baseline. In other words, worship can differ markedly not just from region to region but also within the same city.

That being said, worship components that are reliably present in most services are lighting the chalice, music, joys and sorrows, meditation or prayer, readings, and a sermon.

Lighting the Chalice

The chalice, or flaming chalice, is a powerful symbol for Unitarian Universalists and a ritual that we enact near the beginning of worship. (In this context, a ritual is any symbolic act that focuses our collective attention on a moment in time or that heightens our awareness of the liminal nature of our lives.)

The image of a flame inside of a chalice (an open-cup vessel) eventually gave rise to the action, in worship, of lighting that flame in a physical chalice. Both traditions are relatively young.

The chalice image was created in 1941 by artist Hans Deutsch at the behest of the Unitarian Service Committee as a means of visually conveying their life-saving mission.

That chalice, as a symbol, didn't appear in the context of worship or congregational life until after the Service of Consolidation, in 1963, of the American Unitarian Association and the Universalist Church of America. The large half-chalice jutting out into that ceremonial space clearly inspired some clergy to bring the chalice motif home to the congregations in which they served.

The trend of lighting a chalice was also picked up by UU teenagers in the 1960s, who included the ritual in their conferences. Eventually, the tradition spread throughout our individual congregations, but less like wildfire and more like a creeping vine. It wasn't until the 1980s that the lighting of the chalice became a unifying emblem in our worship life. Today, many Unitarian Universalists consider it an essential marking of sacred space.

Music

"Music stirs something that is beyond words," says Rev. Theresa Novak. "It is the real language of the soul, if the soul has a language at all." For that reason, music is a critical and transcendent component of worship in most UU congregations—"the emotional engine that drives the service," in the words of Rev. Sarah Person.

Just as inspiration for the written word in our worship comes from diverse sources, so does our music. In any given service, you might experience the soaring chords of a Handel oratorio, the bone-deep rhythm of a djembe drum, or a jazz improvisation on brass and keyboard. Our music professionals and other worship leaders choose music that will create the desired mood, becoming what Rev. Joanna Fontaine Crawford calls the "sneaky, sly little bug that creeps past our defenses and touches our feelings even when we think we are in an impenetrable fortress." She adds, "People can resist the message I preach, but they often can't resist the message delivered through great music."

In our worship services, you'll also be invited to sing hymns—traditional or contemporary, sung with sophisticated accompaniment or with none at all—that turn worship into both a collective experience and an embodied one. Many of our leaders use the term "embodied" to remind us, in the words of Theresa Novak, that whether we listen to music or sing, it "resonates with our bodies and the space inside us. The breath, the spirit begins to move within us and around us. We sing and give voice in word and music to our hopes, our dreams, and sometimes to our fears. Depending on the song, we might move or clap. As Unitarian Universalists, we do not believe that the body or the pleasures of the body are sinful. When we sing or dance, we loosen up a bit, get out of our heads, and become connected to our whole selves. One of the hymns in our hymnal contains the line "body and spirit united once more." That, too, is part of our theology.

Joys and Sorrows

In some UU congregations, time is set aside for individuals to name—out loud, in written form, or even silently by lighting a candle—the celebrations or griefs that require the collective attention of the congregation. Many UUs deeply cherish this public sharing of joys and sorrows. For those in grief, the collective witness of that grief can provide healing and comfort. For some, it's a form of intimacy: coming to know one another more deeply beyond our Sunday morning facades.

Meditation or Prayer

There's more variation across the UU landscape with regard to prayer—what it means and how it might happen—than with any other worship element. Even within a single congregation, people will use different terms to refer to the alignment of our full attention with something greater or something internal.

Many people understand meditation as stilling thoughts and deliberately placing intention in the present moment. Lots of practitioners understand meditation as creating a new relationship between you and your mind—becoming the witness. It's the slow, steady, imperfect practice of fostering stillness so that the wisest voice, the most important voices, can emerge from the clatter and chaos between our ears.

The word *prayer*, to some, suggests the participation of a receiver, a listener, another being that's on the other end of our prayers. Many UUs pray to cultivate tenderness in themselves, while others have discovered that prayer can create an internal shift. As renowned theologian Reinhold Niebuhr noted, "Prayer does not change things; prayer changes people, and people change things. . . . Prayer is not hearing voices, prayer is acquiring a voice."

Offering

Unitarian Universalist congregations are self-sustained, supporting their budgets, ministries, and programming from their members' freewill pledges of financial support. In some worship services, the offering is an opportunity to share in that stewardship of the congregation itself, while other congregations designate the offering to a local nonprofit or a UU cause.

Readings

Our Unitarian Universalist worship services, echoing those of our religious ancestors, center on "The Word"—the written or spoken texts that prompt commentary, reflection, or even action. As little as a century ago, that text was scriptural—and it would have been unthinkable to stray beyond those boundaries.

Today, the sources for most UU worship services are limited only by our creativity. Worship leaders might plan a service that includes the work of contemporary poets, science fiction authors, or voices from popular culture. (Sometimes these readings are presented by a worship leader; other times, they're read responsively, as different sections of the congregation give voice to different lines.)

What's more, many congregations use digital media in worship—for example, a slam poetry performance or a music video—to draw wisdom, awe, and contemplative sparks from the world around us. Not only do these forms test traditional expectations of worship but they also often engage listeners at a deeper metaphorical level.

Sermon

It bears repeating: Our ancestors were people of the Word—that is, the Puritans who gave rise to our congregational tradition in the United States centered their worship on God's word as conveyed through scripture. That tradition continues today, as most Unitarian Universalists have come to expect their worship experience to center around the delivery of a sermon, most commonly by a minister. (The difference between a sermon and a homily is that a sermon usually lasts fifteen to twenty minutes, while a homily is around ten minutes or less.)

Regardless of length, the texts and topics that clergy explore in sermons are limited only by their conscience. That's because Unitarian Universalism is a tradition of the free pulpit. Having arisen from Puritan rootstock and congregational autonomy, our faith has long centered on the notion of freedoms *to*: to choose, to question, to think critically, to take risks. Accordingly, our ministers are granted freedom of the pulpit—a principle that's meant to serve the spiritual, ethical, and moral needs of the people.

The flip side of this extraordinary freedom and authority is responsibility: the preacher's ethical and spiritual responsibility to weigh words carefully and to discern when to "comfort the afflicted and afflict the comfortable." Those hearing the sermon, the congregation, also have freedom, the freedom to disagree with the preacher. Rev. Seth Carrier-Ladd affirms that "we encourage everyone 'in the pews' on Sunday morning to filter the sermon against their own beliefs, experiences, and understandings, and then form their own opinion. That opinion may ultimately be in line with the sermon, differ in a few areas, or differ completely. But freedom of the pew is central to what it means to be Unitarian Universalist." Worship isn't defined by consensus on theological questions, and differing opinions are welcome in our congregations; it's *how* those differences are engaged that defines us as Unitarian Universalists.

A Relational People

As with all aspects of congregational life, Unitarian Universalist worship is grounded in covenant, the active process of maintaining relationships of respect and mutuality. Worship is a vessel for the strengthening of our relationships with one another, both as individuals and—from an institutional standpoint—to the people of faith who call themselves UU.

You might say that every element of worship (including those not detailed here) has a relational purpose, serving to connect us to our faith, our values, our purpose, or the sacred mystery in which we all live. Like any relationship, those connections are alive and changing, never fixed. Worship isn't about stasis; ultimately, worship is transformative.

On one hand, people often leave feeling lighter, more at peace, or more hopeful than when they arrived: even within the space of an hour, we can be changed by worshiping in community. On the other hand, the transformative power of worship is also cumulative over long periods of time. Like all relationships of depth, spiritual growth is a journey that invites free-thinking people to reflect, over and over, on life's most demanding questions (and change our answers); wrestle with hurts and, sometimes, the demons that prevent us from feeling whole; or discover our deepest truths.

None of this will be the experience of those who approach worship as consumers or who attend worship casually. These, perhaps, are the two cautionary notes that most Unitarian Universalist ministers place on their abundant and expansive welcome to you.

Rather than centering on individual tastes and preferences, collective worship is, in the words of Rev. Heather Concannon, "an act of generosity and hospitality, not an experience of individualist consumer culture. Even when our own needs or preferences aren't getting met, you can rejoice that your neighbor's need *is* getting met." That is, along with all of the opportunities and invitations inherent to the practice of worship, worship invites us to take up the sometimes challenging but nearly always rewarding demands of being in community.

It's impossible to practice living in community—loving, flawed, diverse, surprising community—without showing up. It's that simple . . . and that complicated, because "show-

ing up" often means choosing to forgo momentary entice-
ments or solitary pursuits by bringing yourself to worship,
week after week (or as often as possible), not because you
might get something out of it but because your presence
might matter to someone else, and because only by gather-
ing together can we create that something larger that has the
capacity to transform us.

A Worship Associate's Testimony

Karen Valbuena

"I could never get up there and do that!" I often hear this reference to public speaking while being thanked for my work as a worship associate. I smile in response, knowing that I can find coffee hour after service more intimidating than public speaking. I am more comfortable connecting with people when I have a role to fulfill. Being a worship associate gives me a role that plays to my strengths and allows me to connect with a lot of people at once.

As part of the team that crafts the Sunday morning service, I now understand how much work it takes to create a meaningful worship experience and how rewarding it is when it all comes together. During the service in my church, the worship associate also shares a short personal reflection on the theme, which I love doing. It's a powerful opportunity to practice being vulnerable and openhearted, trusting in the power of shared experience.

I cherish each time someone reaches out to tell me how they were touched by something I shared. Those heartfelt connections fill me with such joy and truly feed my soul. They also remind me that when it comes down to it, our church community, the work we do and how we do it, is about being in relationship and connecting on a deeper level.

As you explore our UU faith, I hope that you find a place of belonging, a welcoming community and connections that feed your soul.

"Much of ministry
    is a benediction
A speaking well of
    each other and the world
A speaking well of what we value:

honesty
love
forgiveness
trust

A speaking well of our efforts
A speaking well of our dreams

This is how we celebrate life:
through speaking well of it,
living the benediction
and becoming as a word well-spoken."

REV. SUSAN MANKER-SEALE

Our Ministry

Rev. Cheryl M. Walker

Every Sunday, before worship services start, John sweeps the walkways in front of the church. Rain or shine, John is there making sure there is a clear path for people to enter the building. Inside, Agnes is setting up the sanctuary. She checks the microphones, makes sure there are enough candles, and even provides a glass of fresh water for the preacher. Later on, Tess will carefully remove the used candles from the sandbox, knowing that each candle represented something special to the person who lit it. Karla comes early that day; she wants to make sure to get a seat near the windows looking out onto the garden. Her work as a hospice chaplain was especially hard this week, and she needs to be in sacred space with the living, people and trees.

Jeremy is rehearsing the choir. They're still having difficulties with one passage, and he wants them to sound harmonious and glorious during the service, as they usually do. Meanwhile, Mary is sharing the excitement of last week's march for justice in the state capital. She is pleased that so many people responded to her call and showed up, again. Donna is checking the classrooms to see that there are the right supplies for each class and enough teachers for that day. She stops to speak with David and Gabriella, who have been co-teaching the third-grade class this year. Paula arrives with the fresh-baked cookies she makes every week for coffee hour. The youth are delighted by them every time. Bill and Suzy are in the kitchen making coffee. It's the first week of the month, and they always make coffee the first week of the month.

All of these people are doing ministry. Some of them are paid, but most are not. Some do their ministry inside of the church; some do it beyond its walls. Most of them wouldn't think of what they do as ministry but as something they do for their congregation or organization. The one person not mentioned is the person who holds the title of minister. We know that they do ministry, but we should remember that they are not the only ones doing ministry.

Defining Ministry

What is ministry? Simply, it is what we do consistently in order to serve our congregations, our organizations, and our faith, Unitarian Universalism. What distinguishes a ministry from volunteering is that it is done regularly. John sweeps the walkways every Sunday. Mary coordinates social justice in her congregation every week. There is a consistency that makes it a ministry rather than a single volunteer opportunity.

Ministry is done by laypeople, by religious professionals, and by the clergy. Within Unitarian Universalism, we have a concept of shared ministry. We understand that ministry is not the responsibility of a single person in a congregation or an organization, but everyone within the congregation or organization shares it. Everyone is ultimately responsible for the well-being and care of a congregation or Unitarian Universalist organization. There are defined roles and defined levels of authority and power, but ministry has little to do with power and authority; it has to do with service. We share ministry because we share service to our organizations.

Lay Ministries

In our congregations, laypeople perform a myriad of ministries. Some ministries are as simple as being responsible for ensuring there is coffee on Sunday mornings (some people think this is the most important ministry in the congregation). Some are as complicated as serving a term on the board of trustees, creating vision and policies for the congregation. Lay ministries are essential for any congregation to thrive. In most of our congregations, the day-to-day functioning of the congregation is not the responsibility of the laity; it is the responsibility of the staff. However, when laypeople take on ministries within a congregation, the congregation can realize its mission and vision to a much greater extent than when it relegates to its professional staff.

Our social justice ministries are an example of lay ministry making a difference in whether a congregation merely talks about social justice or is actively engaged in its communities doing social justice. Our caring ministries help deepen the connections within a congregation when laypeople are actively involved in the care of the membership. We are stronger, and our lights shine brighter, the more our laity shares the ministry of our congregations and our association.

Religious Professionals

Our religious professionals serving within and beyond our congregations each have unique ministries. Whether they are clergy, religious educators, musicians, administrators, or membership coordinators, their ministries are vital to the health and well-being of Unitarian Universalism. Our religious professionals dedicate themselves to their ministries and the professional exercise of those ministries.

If you participate in a Unitarian Universalist congregation or organization, you can be assured that the people in whom you will place your trust are well trained and are held to a high standard of professional conduct. While the qualifications for religious professionals vary by the type of ministry, all religious professionals are of value to people in the congregations and organizations where they serve. Every professional ministry has an association that, among other things, outlines a professional code of conduct to which its members adhere. Unitarian Universalism is dedicated to ensuring that our religious professionals provide people with the best practices of their ministry. And we believe that it is essential to our present and our future that we honor the work of all of our professional ministries.

Our Clergy

While we recognize that there is shared ministry within our congregations, it is usually the clergy alone who hold the title of minister, though this is changing. In some cases, other religious professionals hold the title of minister, and the clergy may hold a title of pastor. There are no rules about what clergy persons call themselves. Each congregation has a different culture regarding the naming of its clergy. Some have a very informal relationship and call the clergy by first name. Others use the title reverend or doctor as appropriate. Some, usually in the American South, use the title of pastor. However we may name the clergy, theirs is a particular ministry within our congregations and our faith communities.

The other day I was speaking to a member of the congregation where I serve; they remarked that they felt they could share their current struggles with me because when I had asked on Sunday how they were, they knew I meant it. They said to me, "Most people ask but they don't really want to know, but I know that when you ask, you really do want to know. I trust that. I trust you."

At the heart of ministry is *trust*. You should be able to trust your minister. And your minister must work to earn your trust. No one should immediately expect or be granted trust; it is something that must be earned and re-earned through the years. Our clergy earn trust through their training, through the ritual bonding of a minister and a congregation, through their adherence to the highest standards of our practice, and simply through the one-on-one interactions they have with the people where they serve.

Training in Trust

The journey to ordained ministry begins with a call. Something within the person calls them to follow a path that will lead to ordination. Some people hear it when they are young; some hear it later in life. Ministry is a second career for a large percentage of our ministers. For many women, the idea of becoming a minister was not one they thought they could pursue until they were blessed with Unitarian Universalism. This is true for many of our LGBTQ ministers as well. While many other faith communities will not allow women or LGBTQ folks to become ministers, Unitarian Universalism does. In all honesty, it was not easy for us to accept people from the margins into our ministry, and we still have our struggles, but we do not have barriers.

Once a person feels the call to ministry, their formal training and assessment begin. They must go to seminary, which is usually three years. They are required to do an internship, usually but not always, in a congregation. They must do at least one unit of Clinical Pastoral Education, most often by serving as a chaplain in a hospital, where they learn how to be present with people in their most tender of moments. And they must take a battery of psychological exams to be sure they will be capable of performing the duties of ministry. At the end of the road of preparation, there awaits the Ministerial Fellowship Committee, which will assess their fitness for ministry. If all goes well, they will have completed the first part of their training, the first step in earning trust.

Rituals of Trust

The right to ordain is solely the purview of congregations. This is a long tradition from our Unitarian forebears (the Universalists ordained people at their conference meetings). The act of ordination is one of the most important a congregation performs. In the ordination ceremony, a lifelong bond is made between a congregation and a minister that no outside body can break. The congregation, through the act of ordination, says to the world, "We trust this person to be our minister." And the minister makes a commitment to the congregation, that they will always live up to the trust placed in them.

For ministers who will serve in congregations, there is another ritual bond of trust called an installation. It is the right of our congregations to choose their own ministers. Through a selection process, aided by the Unitarian Universalist Association, congregations vote to "call" a minister. Unlike faith traditions with hierarchies, Unitarian Universalism gives each congregation the right to say in whom they will place their trust. When they have decided, there is a ritual during which the minister pledges to uphold the trust put in them by the congregation, and the congregation pledges to treat the minister with respect and fairness.

Building Trust

The trust between a minister and the people of the congregations and organizations where they serve is an ongoing process. Although ministers are trained in seminary, their training does not end there. And while rituals formalize the trusting relationship between a minister and congregation, the ritual alone does not build the bond of trust. The minister must earn the trust every day, so they are continually learning and growing both as a minister and a person. To do that, they need the company and help of other ministers.

Our ministers are expected to be members of the Unitarian Universalist Ministers Association (UUMA), which provides continuing education and collegiality. Additionally, the UUMA has a strong code of professional ethics and conduct to which ministers must adhere. When you trust a minister, you know that they are being held to a high standard of conduct and that the UUMA, along with the UUA, will ensure that they perform to those standards.

Ultimately, the interaction between you and your minister is what truly builds a trusting relationship. Your minister will be there for you when you are in need and when you are celebrating the passages of life. Your minister will be there for you to inspire you to a better life and to help shape a better world. Your minister will be there for you; on that you can place your trust.

We Serve Together

Ministers do ministry, religious professionals do ministry, laypeople do ministry. We all need each other in different ways. Our Unitarian Universalist ministry encompasses a wide variety of gifts and talents. Our congregations are places where we welcome people of good hearts and open minds to find a place for their own ministries.

Julia's staffing of the welcome table is a ministry that invites newcomers to feel right at home the very first time they come. Katie's ministry of caring means everyone who is in the hospital gets a visit and a teddy bear. Mark and Esther's ministry of music brings depth to the worship experience. Greg's administrative ministry keeps everything running smoothly, making space for the creativity of other ministries. Jesse's service on the Board of Trustees is a ministry of vision for the future of her congregation. Then there is Reverend Marie, the minister, head cheerleader, comforter-in-chief, rabble rouser, inspirational speaker, friend in a time of need, keeper of tissues, giver of hugs, toiler in the vineyard of souls.

All are welcome to find their passion and turn it into service to our congregations, our communities, and our Unitarian Universalist faith. All are welcome to discover their ministry.

A Minister's Testimony

Rev. Nic Cable

I was born and raised a Unitarian Universalist, and because of this, I have given my life to its ministry. Extreme? Perhaps. But consider what it gave me. As a young child, I was taught to "be like water" and to admire the flowing river. In this world of sharp lines and divisions, I was taught to celebrate the web of all life that really can and does hold us all. Ours is a religion, I quickly learned, that values growth, change, twists, and turns—we flow on, just like the river; ours is a tradition of flowers blooming and new life breaking forth into the world.

Every day, as a UU minister, I invite people to "be like water," to open their hearts a little wider, to demand justice, and to embody love. The religious community is the embodiment of the love that held me as a child. And now I carry this love and share it with people every day. What else would I give my life to?

"Walk the maze
within your heart: guide your steps into its
    questioning curves.
This labyrinth is a puzzle leading you deeper
    into your own truths.
Listen in the twists and turns.
Listen in the openness within all searching.
Listen: a wisdom within you calls to a wisdom
    beyond you and in that dialogue lies peace."
REV. LESLIE TAKAHASHI

Our Religious Education

Jessica York

Unitarian Universalism invites you on a journey. Unitarian Universalists believe that faith is not static. We believe that the search for meaning in our lives does not call for beliefs that are set and already formed but for beliefs that make sense within our own experiences, wisdom of the world, and our own reason. This is a faith that develops over time, which can morph, organically. Because this is a living faith, expect your experience of it to shift in both depth and breadth. So we speak of faith development as an important aspect of religious life. This is a faith that can accompany you throughout all your life stages, the joys and the sorrows, times of troubling doubt and times of sweet clarity. Yet faith development is not a passive activity. Expect change. UU congregations provide a myriad of ways to engage in faith development. One of the most important of these is through religious education.

Religious education is tool for deepening and widening our faith development. It is not about indoctrination; rather, it provides dedicated time to find ways to distinguish the values that are the foundation of your life and how you can live them more fully. It asks you to find what you want to give your heart to and aids you in taking concrete steps to do so. It provides a brave space for you to ask the questions you need to ask, both big and small. *Is there a God? What happens when we die? How do I live a life of integrity? How do I love my neighbor in a world full of fear, anger, and division?* Religious education programs bring people together to support each other in the work of making meaning of their lives.

A Lifelong Journey

Unitarian Universalist congregations affirm and promote seven Principles, which individual Unitarian Universalists hold as strong values and moral guides. The third Principle says UU congregations affirm and promote acceptance of one another and encouragement to spiritual growth in our congregations. This affirmation of spiritual growth is why religious education is crucial to our faith. We are believers in lifelong learning, not just in academic matters but in matters of the heart and the spirit. Our religious education programs start in early childhood and continue throughout our lives. Religious educators hold responsibility for programs in most congregations. They provide space for people of different ages to explore life's questions and how we live out the answers.

Our religious education programs are places where you can deepen your understanding of the values you hold dear and how those values affect the decisions you make in your day-to-day life. Whether you are a youth in a small-group ministry session sharing and listening to stories of how white privilege affects people of color and white people, a child involved in a photo documentary project on family diversity in the congregation, or an elder reflecting upon spiritual ancestors who have influenced your life, our religious education programs encourage you to ask the questions you uniquely need to ask and seek the answers only you can give.

UU religious education programs help you find the answers in workshops full of stories and activities from the many Sources Unitarian Universalists find inspiring: direct experience, humanist teachings, the words of prophetic people, and wisdom from the world's religions, including those from Judaism and Christianity (with which we share historic roots) and from earth-centered religions, past and present. You will find religious education opportunities in groups of similarly aged people and in multigenerational groups. Multigenerational learning acknowledges that wisdom can come to us from people of any age and is crucial to building the beloved community. Middle school youth sharing their credo statements of belief from their Coming of Age program is a way that all ages can understand something about how young people are experiencing today's world. Middle-aged adults leading preschoolers in meditation enables the sharing of gifts and sends a message that spiritual practices can help anyone at any age stay centered in an overly busy world.

The Path of the Journey

Just as each individual has a unique faith journey, each congregation and covenanted UU community has unique religious education programming. Unitarian Universalism, as a creedless religion, is a faith where not everyone is expected to profess the same beliefs or prescribe to a particular orthodoxy. Because we see faith as a journey, we understand that it can change as we age, have new experiences, and meet and engage respectfully with people who hold different ideas from our own.

Most congregations offer religious education programming on Sunday morning, but you might find offerings any time during the week. A professional religious educator may be responsible for programming, possibly assisted by a committee and a dedicated group of volunteer teachers. Classes may be designed for specific ages (preschool, children, middle school, high school, young adults, adults, older adults) or may be multi-age, incorporating material oriented toward a specific interest (nature, Bible study, Unitarian Universalist history). We believe that a cycle of teaching and learning characterizes the best educational formats, so teachers come ready to learn from participants and participants understand that they are welcome to bring the knowledge they already possess. Therefore, workshops are interactive, experiential, and kinesthetic, engaging different learning styles and pedagogies.

Religious education programming often involves the use of curricula. The Unitarian Universalist Association has a series of core curricula for ages preschool through older adulthood. Tapestry of Faith is a collection of curricula and resources that nurture Unitarian Universalist identity, spiritual growth, a transforming faith, and vital communities of justice and love. The vision for Tapestry of Faith supports lifespan learning outcomes across four strands: ethical development, faith development, spiritual development, and Unitarian Universalist identity. Free, online, and immensely adaptable, a religious educator can tailor programming to suit the particular needs of their unique UU community. Each program has a distinct topic; some examples of topics include what it means to belong to a faith home, a deep exploration of our Principles and Sources, ethical decision making, stories from the Hebrew and Christian scriptures, world religions, best practices in interfaith work, and the miracles of science and nature.

Every program within Tapestry of Faith includes opportunities for justice making in the congregation, local community, or the wider world. Unitarian Universalists believe that working for justice is a faithful activity and that we are all responsible for helping to create a better world. Guided by values of compassion, empathy, integrity, courage, and love, we understand the need to learn about the root causes and history of injustice, in addition to taking action. Factoring in time for reflection helps you connect social justice activities to your Unitarian Universalist faith and the meaning you make of your life in the context of the rest of the world. Religious education provides both background and foreground for justice and witnessing.

Tapestry of Faith programs also provide opportunities for spiritual practice. Walking into a religious education workshop, you may see preschoolers planting and nurturing a garden, kindergartners walking a labyrinth in silence, a seventh grader creating a mandala, a high school youth journaling, or a young adult reading a prayer they wrote in a poetry slam. We know that our spirits are nourished in many different ways. There are other ways to experience spiritual practices in addition to participation in religious education programs. Worship is one of those. Some congregations offer classes in yoga, meditation, singing, or other activities. Daily readings from the UUA's Worship Web is one way an individual can bring more spirituality into their lives, as are the weekly reflections offered via email by Braver/Wiser. Our religious education programs allow all ages to sample different practices, seeking the ones that feel right to them, and encourage participants to include spiritual practices in their regular schedules.

Accompanying You on the Journey

Ubuntu is a concept that comes to us from the Bantu people of southern Africa. Archbishop Desmond Tutu of South Africa says the word can mean "My humanity is inextricably bound up in yours." In community, we experience the full range of what it means to be human. The values and principles we claim are meaningless unless they are practiced in community. In our UU communities, we come together as people of faith to do the hard work of living our values. It can be messy and we will make mistakes; yet, community life is the practicum of all the reflections and discussions from the religious education programs.

It is comforting to know that we are not alone in this faith journey of deepening and widening our spirits. We join in the community of the faithful to have our values affirmed and challenged. We come to build relationships and hear stories that are different from our own. What we learn from direct experience with each other is at least as important as anything we learn in a religious education curriculum. Our religious education programs are full of people with diverse identities: many ethnicities, races, genders, abilities, and sexual orientations. They are a microcosm of the world we need to live and thrive in. We practice our faith most fully when we do so with those who may be different from us and still possess inherent worth and dignity.

Religious education opportunities are not confined to the walls of the congregational building or to Sunday morning. Programs may be offered on weeknights and afternoons. Social justice actions are great opportunities for religious education, so do not be surprised if, after a march for racial justice, you are invited to sit and process the activity with other participants or to write a reflection piece for the congregational newsletter. On Wednesday night, young people might gather at a neighboring congregation for a session on gender identity from Our Whole Lives, the UU comprehensive sexuality program. On Saturday afternoon, a religious educator might conduct a workshop on life planning at a retirement community. Families from a homeschooling co-op might use a session from Building Bridges: A World Religions Program to learn more about Islam.

Religious education programs consider it a responsibility to support families at home. You may hear the term *family ministry* used to refer to services and materials for use at home. Parents and caregivers are children's first and primary religious educators. Children will learn a great deal about faith and values from their interactions with their families. After all, they spend much more time with family members than they do at the congregation. Religious educators see themselves in partnerships with parents and caregivers. They value the time, talent, and ideas that parents, caregivers, and children bring to the program. They provide tools for continued conversations and explorations after Sunday School has ended, such as the Families pages in *UUWorld* magazine, Taking It Home Handouts from Tapestry of Faith curricula, books of stories from our UU history, and scouting material to aid in meeting the requirements for Religion in Life badges. Families of all configurations and sizes, with or without children, related by blood or chosen, are a welcome part of this family ministry.

A Journey of Transformation

Being part of a multigenerational community . . .

Having a place where you can ask questions freely and without shame . . .

Designating time to reflect upon how our values affect our lives . . .

All of these are good reasons to participate in religious education programming. Yet, in and of themselves, they are not the goal. The ultimate goal of religious education is transformation. As Unitarian Universalists, we realize that we are imperfect beings. Always we can do better: be more empathetic; show up more often for justice; care for the sick, the lonely, the brokenhearted; and create more love in the world. We are a long way from creating the heaven on earth we all desire. How do we get to that place? If there were easy answers, we would be there already. Yet, each day, we can use our lives to go about the work of transforming the world into a place of peace and love. But, as Unitarian Universalist and consultant on multicultural organizations Paula Cole Jones says, "You cannot transform the world without being transformed yourself."

Our religion does not ask you to be born again. We are instead challenged to bring all that we *already are*—our identities, life experiences, failures and fears, hopes and dreams—and to go on a journey of transformation. If your religion is not helping you to be a better person, what good is it? There is no original sin here. You will not be asked to confess sins weekly or to wear a hair shirt. Yet, this is a place where you can admit to your imperfections, knowing that instead of making you less human they actually make you more so. We all live our highest values imperfectly, and we can all commit to do better. In religious education programs, you will hear stories of those courageous enough to live lives with purpose, and you will share how their story relates to yours. Parents and givers will share how they are trying to guide their children in the ways of compassion. Children will learn ways to confront bullies. Elders will reflect upon the legacy they wish to leave.

An important aspect of transformation is ritual. Rituals help us mark the transitions that transformation brings. Religious education workshops include everyday rituals, like lighting a chalice, singing UU hymns, or building an altar. Religious education programs celebrate new life with child dedications. They offer coming of age and bridging workshops to mark young people's journey in faith, and they may offer sage-ing retreats to recognize the changing nature of our faith that lasts even into elderhood.

Author T. S. Eliot said, "We shall not cease from exploration. And the end of all our exploring will be to arrive where we started and know the place for the first time." This is the nature of the transformation offered by Unitarian Universalist religious education programs: a constant re-knowing of our hearts, our spirits, and ourselves. All of this is what a religious education program can offer you along your faith journey. May you journey well.

A Religious Educator's Testimony

Joy Berry

As a professional religious educator, I am committed to cultivating the development of faith among Unitarian Universalists. This is no simple task; growing faith is more practice and process than prediction or product, more art and story than exact science.

The work of religious education is a ministry. It is fulfilling, yet it is also messy, and at times, it is deeply challenging. Despite the complexity, I am drawn to this essential work in a way I can only describe as a calling.

I believe faith development is essential because it inspires us to seek justice and find compassion and helps us craft creative solutions to human problems both old and new. It stirs our spirits toward hope and wholeness and makes room for grace. It helps us name and claim the stories that have shaped us as individuals and then carries us, when we need it most, toward covenant and community. Faith development, in short, transforms—and even saves—lives.

I see myself as an accomplice and ally to that sacred process, even as it helps me see that I too am still in formation, as we all should be. As a religious educator, I have

set my heart, mind, and hands to supporting our shared
work as Unitarian Universalists: to keep growing in faith,
together.

"The choice to bless the world is more than an act
     of will
a moving forward into the world
with the intention to do good.
It is an act of recognition,
a confession of surprise,
a grateful acknowledgment
that in the midst of a broken world
unspeakable beauty, grace and mystery abide….
None of us alone can save the world.
Together—that is another possibility, waiting."

REV. REBECCA ANN PARKER

Our Work for Social Justice

Rev. Elizabeth Nguyen

The Unitarian Universalist feminist and peace activist Margaret Moseley called social justice work moving mountains, one stone at a time. Margaret was born in Boston in 1910. She dreamed of being a nurse, but being African American, she was turned away from all of the nursing schools in the city. She went on to help found Cooperative Way and Freedom House and to lead the anti-McCarthyism movement and the Community Church of Boston.

We move mountains, one stone at a time; as Unitarian Universalists, our journey is to transform the big and the small, to transform ourselves, and to transform the world. Universalism means no one is outside of the circle of love and no one is disposable. We stubbornly seek out the spark of the divine in each other, no matter what. Interdependence means none of us is truly free until we are all free, and our thriving is bound up in the earth's thriving. We struggle for liberation from the violence of white supremacy, sexism, ableism, classism, and heterosexism. Our covenants mean we make promises to our communities to honor love and justice above all else.

Unitarian Universalism is there, in the youth group at the Pride Parade, covered in rainbows and glitter. Unitarian Universalism is there, in the climate activist on trial for doing what she sees as necessary to return to a right relationship with the earth. Unitarian Universalism is there, in the congregation providing space, childcare, and dinner for the coalition organizing after the police killing of a young person. Unitarian Universalism is there, in the justice team that accompanies an undocumented person to her court dates, raises money for her legal fees, and builds community with her family.

Unitarian Universalism is for those who have seen the arc bend toward justice and those who doubt it will ever bend but know we must organize as if our lives depend on it anyway, because they do. Some theologies say that only some people are saved. From those theologies flows a world where people are criminalized for their identities—for being Muslim, transgender, Black, undocumented. Our theology says that we are all saved, and salvation is what we strive to build now, for each other. So we resist any laws, policies, or practices that deny anyone their humanity. We know that now on earth is our chance to create heaven. We know that love crosses borders and prison walls, lives in queer families and disability justice organizers, thrives among trans young people and working-class elders.

Some religions think of suffering as something that happens to individuals, which individuals must heal from. As Unitarian Universalists, we know suffering is also collective. And that we heal collectively. The original wounds of slavery and genocide in this country cannot be fully repaired in any one individual life. Instead, we work for collective healing and liberation.

Our Unitarian Universalist justice ancestors like Margaret Moseley remind us that we are not alone and that we come from a long legacy of healing and repair. Our legacy includes those who have sacrificed for justice and those who have been cowardly in the face of injustice. We know that behind the struggles for the abolition of slavery, for voting rights, for LGBTQ justice that can look so pretty in the newspapers, there is messiness, betrayal, falling short, and the seduction of choosing comfort over convictions.

Unitarian Universalism is there, too, reckoning with all the ways we have broken our vows and all of our imperfection. With the parent trying to figure out how to get through the day and show up for that community meeting. With those of us who are white, trying to speak up and act out against white supremacy and also love ourselves and our families. With those of us who are people of color, trying to unapologetically live our values, knowing the cost that can come to our careers and our spirits. We are already saved from perfection. And Unitarian Universalist community, songs, prayers, and spiritual practices are there to remind us when we forget.

For me, it's singing. Because when I'm singing, I'm breathing. When I'm terrified that the meeting is going to fall apart, when someone I trust and look up to is giving me feedback that's hard to hear, or when I'm about to knock on someone's door or engage in direct action or sit down with the elected official or write the grant, that's when I try to remember that I can sing.

Don't get me wrong: I'm not a good singer. But it's not about being a good singer. It's about remembering that singing brings me back to courage, possibility, and enough space for spirit.

Practicing under Pressure

Unitarian Universalism is a community of people practicing together. We practice living our values, not just on Sunday mornings or on our best days. We practice embodying our deepest truths under pressure, when our backs are against the wall. This is a thorny spiritual truth—that who we are on our worst days is who we actually are.

Organizer Caitlin Breedlove often says that we respond to crisis with our highest level of training, not with our highest values. Buddhist teacher Rev. angel Kyodo williams writes that "today's progressive leaders must systematically and lovingly prepare us to tolerate the inherent discomfort of change now in order to wedge open the way to transformation in the future. They must do this under pressure; they must do this while in motion; and they must do this with and on behalf of others."

Pressure reveals to me where I am so practiced. And where I have never done this before. Or to say it another way, pressure reveals to me where I embody my values—they are not separate from me—and where they are the first things I forget about. Some people say we have to do a new thing twenty-one times for it to become a new pattern of behavior, three hundred times for it to become instinct, three thousand times for personal transformation, and ten thousand times for mastery.

Whatever we practice, we get really great at. If we practice flexibility, humility, courage, we get strong at those things. If we practice rigidness, ego, cowardice, we get strong at those things. If we practice saying no one ever trained me to do that or we don't have enough or I'm afraid to try, that muscle gets more and more practiced.

When my father's family came to the United States as refugees from Vietnam, a woman named Ruth in Wisconsin opened her home and welcomed them. Ruth had somehow gotten enough practice living her values under pressure that she was willing to have her family's life transformed by mine. There is a thing that happens for so many of us: that some things are news and other things are family. For some of us, increased Islamophobia is news. For some of us, increased Immigration and Customs Enforcement or surveillance of activists or stop-and-frisk or addiction or climate chaos or cash bail are issues or headlines. For some of us, it's family.

As Unitarian Universalists, we live our values because they are morally right but also because we know that we are family. And we are going to fight for each other like family because, in the end, if we believe in our words about interdependence, they actually are.

So we practice together. That it is not our first or second time trying to live our values under pressure. We will practice at least the three thousand times needed to embody our values in our communities.

The Hard Way

I once saw a little sign, carved in wood, that read, "There is only the hard way." Many of us have been harmed by theology that told us that suffering was a sacrifice that would bring us closer to God. Many of us were told that our suffering would redeem us. Even when we knew that actual redemption would have been to be free from the suffering to begin with. And many of us are only here because of the sacrifices of others. So much of what is possible to carve out in this world requires some giving up, some letting go, some sacrifice.

That is the truth of that little wooden sign: there is no easy way. There is only the hard way. In particular, the work of justice often asks us to do impossible, hard, terrifying things. There is no easier way. There is only this one hard way. Folks with more privilege sometimes get caught up here. "If it's hard, maybe we are doing it wrong," we tell ourselves. We are lulled by our experiences of choosing between a hard choice and an easier one. Folks with less privilege know that many of our choices are between a horrific choice and a horrific choice. And we learn to live with that and keep going.

Many of us want to do the right thing, the just thing, the generous thing, and also not have to give anything at all. We want to share our opinions but not actually donate our evenings, our weekends, our doing-dishes-while-on-the-conference-call to get to understand the work enough to be able to offer meaningful thoughts. We want people to trust us and let us shape the vision but not actually risk inviting folks out to tea, dinner, beers, or church to build a relationship that endures and carries us forward. We may want to post the cute meme without actually making the phone call to the city councilor or state representative. We want to be part of that powerful, courageous, game-changing, direct action without the long-past-midnight planning meetings, the messy decision making, the frayed relationships, and the constant wondering if this is even worth it. We want to talk about being bound together in interdependence but do not actually want to give our guest room to a stranger, give a paycheck to someone we've never met, or turn our schedule inside out to do what needs to be done.

The word *sacrifice* might be too much mess for some of us, too tainted by oppression and coercion. What matters more is that we are willing to live our lives in the shape of what is being asked, not hope that what we are asked to do will fit the shape of our lives. When we believe that the work of justice should fit our lives, instead of being willing to let our lives move to fit it, we cede so much of our power.

I can't unknow the sacrifices that my parents, my grandparents, and my ancestors made for me. I can wish they weren't necessary or that there had been another way, but that's an alternate world. In this one, what others have done for me becomes fuel for figuring out how to "keep moving with your heart hurt and your body starting to tire," as Toshi Reagon sings. One of the principles of Movimiento Cosecha is sacrifice: "Our seeds come from the tree of sacrifice. We honor the hard work of all the people who bring their gifts to the movement. We believe that people's work in Cosecha is for the collective well-being of everyone and not for personal gain or to advance individual interests." Mary Hooks, in her work leading Southerners On New Ground, offers this mandate: "to avenge the suffering of our ancestors, to earn the respect of future generations, and to be transformed in the service of the work."

As Unitarian Universalists, we lean into the hard questions: What do we value that we are willing to let go for something we value even more? What must we do to earn the respect of those who come after? What is the hard way we are willing to go?

Humility

What about when we disagree? It happens, all of the time. You have probably read some things here that you have disagreed with. We know that our religious ancestors disagreed. Communities fractured over the abolition of slavery and integration, just as others were strong and united in their convictions. Our spiritual communities are full of big and little disagreements—from what to put on our banners to what role religious people and communities should play in the work of justice.

Our spiritual muscles are what allow us to stay in community across difference, differentiate the fake disagreements from the real ones, and sort out when to be humble about what we might not understand and when to be unwavering in what we know to be true. In the journey of justice, just like the journey of the spirit, we know that new truths are always being revealed. And we know that spiritual truths persist that we must never compromise. Harm to any being is harm to the web of all life. While there are absolutely wrong behaviors, there are no wrong people. The circle of love holds us all.

As Rev. Rosemary Bray McNatt has written, "The truth is this: If there is no justice, there will be no peace . . . if we cannot bring justice to the small circle of our own individual lives, we cannot hope to bring justice to the world. And if we do not bring justice to the world, none of us is safe and none of us will survive. Nothing that Unitarian Universalists need to do is more important than making justice real—here, where we are."

Activists' Testimony

Susan and Mac Goekler

We came to a passion for social justice work separately and found it cemented our relationship. Although not born to wealth, we were both born to privilege and recognize that our blessings should be used for the benefit of all, not just ourselves. Unitarian Universalists believe in the "inherent worth and dignity of all." How can you believe that and not respond when you see suffering or injustice? Our UU faith has given us the grounding needed to stay committed, even in the absence of observable progress. We have seen people give up on social justice work out of frustration. Frustration is what keeps us at the table. Many people live hand to mouth, while many of us live good lives. We consider it a moral calling to work toward making the world a better place.

Our participation in UU congregations has put us in touch with people willing to work together for justice and compassion. UUs have different social justice passions—some work toward racial justice, some toward protecting the environment, some on relieving poverty, some on creating a more peaceful world, plus, plus. We don't have to agree on issues or solutions, but we have found emotional, theological, social, and logistical support for our work in our UU church community.

"We seek to be a home for all who desire our company.

We seek to make a welcome for all those in search of our good news

Come, come, little children, teens, young adults, adults, and elders.

Come, families in great diversity.

Come to this loving home and safe harbor—but not to find a place to escape the world.

This is a community of engagement—and of creativity.

We come together to create boldly—dangerously.

We must create the Beloved Community with an awareness of how difficult it is—because it is hard work. It is work that challenges us to bring our whole selves and engage deeply and for the long haul.

Our faith, our tradition, must call us into community. Our task is to create spaces where we might know and value each other.

We must listen to our stories."

ADAPTED FROM REV. NATALIE MAXWELL FENIMORE

Our Communities

Aisha Hauser

Unitarian Universalists are uniquely positioned to create atmospheres where people can learn from each other about the most difficult of topics. I love this faith. Everyone should have a place that affirms their being, that declares they are loved in the fullness of who they are. The way I explain Unitarian Universalism to folks is, "We all came from one source and we are all loved." If anyone asks me to elaborate, I talk about my interfaith family and our desire to be part of a pluralist community whose members work toward a society that lives out justice and equity in all forms.

All of the world's religions struggle through what it means to be human. Many faiths promise returns in the afterlife for earthly struggles. Unitarian Universalists struggle with what it means to be human right here and right now, with no promises of what may or may not happen after we die. It seems that for us to learn how to work toward social justice on a national scale, it would serve us to learn to do it internally in our own congregations.

Unitarian Universalist congregations offer opportunities to engage in justice work as part of how we interact and engage with how we are in community. There is a sentiment that I read in a book about Zen teachings that I try to live by: "How you do anything is how you do everything." If we are going to work for justice in our world, what does it look like to work for it in our own UU congregations? Do we recognize and respond to ways to promote justice work in our liberal faith communities? When we do, we can exercise our "justice muscles" with regard to how to bring change. It is not easy to speak truth to power when that truth is in our own spaces and when the power consists of our friends on the board or our own minister.

I have been a UU religious educator for more than fifteen years. I've seen examples of UUs using their agency to bring change within their congregation. At East Shore Unitarian Church in Bellevue, Washington, both the middle school and high school youth groups were the catalyst for social justice work that impacted the congregation as a whole. In 2015, members of the high school youth group asked that the weekly response to the chalice lighting said during worship change to be more inclusive by not using gender binary language. The chalice response had referenced "brothers and sisters"; instead, the youth asked the adults in charge to change these references to "siblings in spirit." The senior minister, board president, and I discussed the matter and decided that the wording would be changed and that the youth group would be invited to talk to the congregation about why this change is part of being an inclusive community. The youth group did this, and the congregation has been using more inclusive language ever since.

One year later, the middle school youth group, inspired by Tapestry of Faith programs, embarked on a project to raise money to retrofit water fountains so water bottles can be filled. The group sold stainless steel water bottles to the entire congregation and informed them about their efforts to raise awareness about the need to reduce plastic water bottle usage because our water sources are threatened by pollution and other factors. The middle schoolers were successful in their fund-raising efforts, and two water fountains were retrofitted. The youth in both these examples identified a challenge within the congregation and worked to address it.

The Our Whole Lives sexuality education program is another way to live out social justice by teaching people of all ages about their own self-esteem, consent, and how to embrace and love themselves. This is a form of social justice that will always be an integral part of empowerment for children and youth who are learning who they are and how to interact in a healthy way with others. The youth programs especially affirm what a healthy relationship entails and how to recognize when someone exhibits behaviors of abuse. Issues of social media use and abuse are reflected on and considered so that youth are encouraged to view their digital footprint through a social justice lens.

Our Whole Lives affirms gender fluidity and all sexual orientations. Beginning with the kindergarten–first-grade program, children and their parents are given tools to talk to each other about sexuality in a healthy and clear way. Children who grow up with a healthy attitude toward their bodies and sexuality are more secure and more likely to talk to their parents when they have questions. Children and youth who identify as part of the LGTBI community are held in love and affirmed in their wholeness. Parents are supported in our congregations to be allies to their children and youth. In a time when misinformation about those in the LGBTI community is widespread, offering ways to present clear, factual, and life-affirming programs within our faith community is social justice work.

One area where Unitarian Universalism has the potential to help influence and impact the national conversation is race. White Unitarian Universalists have perspectives that illustrate a full spectrum of understanding of racial dynamics that have shaped this nation since its founding. What is also crucial to growing spiritually with regard to racial justice is connecting the dots of our statements to our actions.

Congregations across the denomination have been having intentional and difficult conversations about how to transform into truly inclusive places. This has not been easy; there have been people who resist the idea that we need to do anything differently. More inspiring are those, including the Unitarian Universalist Association president, Rev. Susan Frederick-Gray, who are committed to doing better, listening to those on the margins, and affirming that we must be a faith that remains relevant by asking the difficult and challenging questions of ourselves.

Currently, the national conversation includes race, power, and what it means to be a multicultural nation. Our human disposition is to gravitate to those we feel are similar to ourselves, but our opportunity is to live out values of mutual respect. My life's work is to empower people to engage in difficult conversations in order to achieve common understanding of differing opinions, while also acknowledging the power differentials that exist in our society.

As an immigrant born in Alexandria, Egypt, I've lived in five different states and three different countries. I've met, worked, and made friends with people from all over the world, in three languages. This has helped me understand what drives people and how fear plays a role in how we respond to rapid changes as well as how building relationships fosters mutual respect and care. What drives me most is to help create a world that accepts all multiethnic, multicultural children in all their complex fullness. Through UU faith development, we could create a holistic infrastructure to model what it means to live in a diverse, pluralist society.

I am proud to be a Unitarian Universalist. We struggle together to understand what it is to be human and how we can take responsibility for changing injustice when we recognize it, both within our faith and in the larger world.

This is an exciting time to be Unitarian Universalist. The first elected female president of the Unitarian Universalist Association has committed to shared ministry and to listening to those who ache to be a part of a life-affirming faith.

We have opportunities for folks with marginalized identities to be part of UU affinity groups, like the following:

Diverse Revolutionary Unitarian Universalist Multicultural Ministries (DRUUMM) is a ministry centered on the needs of all who identify as people of color. Gatherings are planned in different regions throughout the year.

Black Lives of Unitarian Universalism (BLUU) is a ministry by Black UUs for Black UUs. For the first time in the history of our faith, Black UUs are being centered and loved in their wholeness.

EqUUal Access is Unitarian Universalists living with disabilities, their families, friends, and allies coming together for a common purpose: to enable the full engagement of people with disabilities in Unitarian Universalist communities and the broader society.

Cultural paradigm shifts are uncomfortable for most people, and UUs aren't immune to that discomfort. As in any community, we sometimes fall short by resisting change, falling into defensiveness, and at times retreating into denial. The road to spiritual maturity is in struggle and working through pain, and our faith calls us to mutual support in humility and curiosity as we do the work together. Our faith is continually grappling with how to live out our values authentically and with integrity. This is the gift of our faith. We do this without mandates of archaic ideas but as part of a living tradition that believes that revelation is not sealed.

A Lay Leader's Testimony

Karla Baehr

I've learned that doing "committee work" in a UU community can and must be—at its core—spiritual work. Our covenant demands that I try to bring my most grateful and generous self to it. A UU congregation is like a laboratory where I can practice certain ways of being and doing and then try to bring them into the wider world—at home, at work, in the community. I can offer gifts I'm confident about, try out ones that are far less developed, and seek out and celebrate the gifts of others.

My committee work has sustained, strengthened, and connected me. It has also sometimes stretched me out of my comfort zone: asking for money as a member of the annual pledge drive team or having my assumptions challenged on the planning team for congregation-wide conversations on implicit bias and racism.

At my congregation, we've established rituals like chalice lightings and check-ins to open meetings. This helps to remind us of the spiritual nature of even the most mundane board or committee work. And we close most meetings standing in a circle, looking each other in the eye, and saying together, "Thank you for helping us do together what we cannot do alone!" I'm left grounded and grateful.

"Because of those who came before, we are;
in spite of their failings, we believe;
Because of, and in spite of the horizons of their
vision,
we, too, dream."

REV. BARBARA PESCAN

Our Roots

Dan McKanan

Unitarian Universalists possess a rich heritage and many different ways of relating to it. Some argue that because we lack a shared theology, it is our common history that holds us together. Others relish the freedom to draw on multiple spiritual sources without being bound to any single tradition. Some take pride in knowing that unitarian and universalist ideas (notice the small "u"s) are as old as Christianity itself. Our "free and responsible search for truth and meaning" is more ancient still. Others stress the distinctly American flavor of our movement, noting that Unitarianism and Universalism (capital "U"s) were born in the epoch of the Revolution. Still others tell the stories of our partner churches in Transylvania, the British Isles, the Khasi Hills of India, and the Philippines, insisting that their histories are our heritage as well.

Ancient Roots

Given this diversity, one might begin telling the Unitarian Universalist story at many different points in time. UU Buddhists and UU Pagans claim a heritage that is older than Christianity. But most Unitarian Universalists trace their roots to the biblical traditions of Judaism and Christianity. The ideas of "unitarianism," that God is one being, and "universalism," that God will save all humanity, can be found in the scriptures of ancient Judaism. For millennia, Jews have declared daily that "the Lord is one" and cherished the hope that "all the families of the earth shall be blessed."

These beliefs were part of the rich diversity of early Christianity. Searching the scriptures, some theologians found hope that all humans and even the devil would be restored to harmony with the divine. The official church refused to teach that this was certainly so. Yet Catholic and Eastern Orthodox theologians continue to teach it as a possibility. The idea of unitarianism was much more controversial. As the Roman Empire was becoming Christian, church leaders declared that Jesus Christ, the Holy Spirit, and God the Father were a Trinity, sharing a single divine substance. Those who found this unbiblical or too paradoxical created a rival church, with its own hierarchy and dogmas. Even after that church died out, unitarianism was despised as a heresy by most Christians.

Unitarianism experienced renewal at the time of the Protestant Reformation, in the sixteenth century. Protestants cherished the principle of *sola scriptura*. They relied entirely on the text of the Bible. Those who took this principle furthest rejected the idea of a state church, insisting that Christians should choose voluntarily to follow Christ's path. Among their modern descendents are the Amish and Mennonites. One small wing of this movement also rejected the idea of a Trinity as unbiblical. They planted churches first in Poland and then Transylvania, where a Unitarian king embraced a policy of religious freedom.

The Polish church eventually disappeared, while Transylvanian Unitarianism survives today. Unitarian ideas reappeared in seventeenth- and eighteenth-century England and Ireland. Those who held them, including the philosopher John Locke, blended a commitment to biblical authority with the Enlightenment's stress on reason. Unlike the deists on one side and orthodox Christians on the other, they refused to choose between reason and revelation. Their first congregation was the Essex Street Chapel. Organized in 1774 by a former Anglican priest named Theophilus Lindsey, it set the tone for similar congregations in the American colonies. Universalist ideas were also promoted in England during these years, first by Gerrard Winstanley, founder of the socially radical Diggers during the English Civil War. Later in the seventeenth century, Jane Leade and the Philadelphia Society linked universal salvation to mystical visions of paradise restored. A century later, revivalist James Relly taught universalism on the grounds that Christ had died to save not individuals but all humanity as a single body.

American Founding

Though European movements influenced their North American sisters, the origin of Universalism and Unitarianism in the United States did not involve the transplanting of European institutions to new soil. Nor was there a single "founding moment" for either tradition. Several different groups held unitarian or universalist beliefs. They came together only gradually.

The first people in North America to teach universal salvation may have been Germans who came to Pennsylvania for religious freedom. Their mystical Christianity also inspired them to live in celibate community, practice alchemy, and wait for the end of the world. The first explicitly Universalist congregation was planted in Gloucester, Massachusetts, by John Murray, an English immigrant who had learned from James Relly that an all-powerful God had predestined everyone to be saved. But the largest number of early Universalists came out of Baptist churches in western New England. Skeptical of educated ministers, they read the Bible for themselves and cherished debates with neighbors who read it differently. These diverse communities began to organize a General Convention in 1790. They had little in common other than their belief in universal salvation and a fierce opposition to state-sponsored religion. This put them in conflict with the Puritan or "Standing Order" congregations of New England, which received tax support well into the nineteenth century.

The first Unitarian congregations in the United States were inspired by Englishman Joseph Priestley. Priestley was a chemist who discovered oxygen, a friend of Thomas Jefferson, and a theologian who insisted that Jesus was no more than human. In 1784, his writings convinced the minister of King's Chapel in Boston to eliminate references to the Trinity from that congregation's liturgy. Ten years later, Priestley immigrated to the United States and helped found congregations in Philadelphia and rural Pennsylvania.

Like the Universalists, Priestley was wary of state-sponsored religion. But ironically, several Standing Order churches in the neighborhood of Boston embraced a milder form of Unitarianism. They believed that Jesus was more than human but less than divine. They also stressed the goodness of humanity. While their Puritan ancestors had seen humans as depraved, they had absorbed the optimistic Enlightenment philosophy taught at Harvard College. The debate over these new ideas caused a schism among the churches in Massachusetts. Though the Unitarians were reluctant to separate from their more orthodox brothers and sisters, they created the American Unitarian Association in 1825.

Each fledgling denomination had a theological champion. The Universalists' Hosea Ballou was a fiery debater who delighted in clever interpretations of the Bible. He taught that Jesus had died not to appease an angry God but to soften the hard hearts of humanity. And he took the radical position that even the worst sinners will go straight to heaven. Other Universalists speculated that some would be purified by temporary hellfire.

The Unitarians' William Ellery Channing was a reluctant radical. He loved peace and helped organize opposition to the War of 1812. He hesitated to organize a separate denomination but eventually became its most eloquent spokesman. He also hesitated to speak out against slavery. When abolitionist friends persuaded him to join their cause, he found himself alienated from the wealthy congregation he had served for decades.

Though Channing was a Unitarian and Ballou a Universalist, each man appreciated aspects of the other tradition. Ballou was a proud champion of Priestleyan unitarianism. Channing was not a universalist, but his faith in the human capacity to grow in likeness to the divine drew on the same spiritual streams as ancient universalism. The two men scarcely acknowledged one another, though they ministered in the same Boston neighborhood. Today's Arlington Street Church is heir to both of their congregations.

Ministers were not the only people who helped build up the two traditions. John Murray's wife, Judith Sargent Murray, was a powerful leader and advocate of women's rights. She began demanding equal access to education in 1779 and composed the first Universalist catechism three years later. Lucy Barnes was disabled by asthma but wrote letters to spread the Universalist faith. Catharine Sedgwick, one of the nation's most popular writers, incorporated Unitarian themes into her novels. Unitarian Hannah Adams expressed her liberal religious convictions in one of the first dictionaries of world religions.

Heretics, Reformers, and Institution Builders

Three different sorts of leaders helped nineteenth-century Unitarianism and Universalism evolve. First, there were the heretics—unfettered thinkers who reached beyond inherited theologies. Abner Kneeland, who called himself a pantheist rather than a Christian, left the Universalist ministry to lead Boston's Society of Free Enquirers. He was the last person jailed for blasphemy in the United States. Ralph Waldo Emerson shocked the faculty of Harvard Divinity School by urging future ministers to preach from their own souls rather than from scripture. The Transcendentalist movement he launched transformed American literature as well as the Unitarian ministry. During the 1850s, roughly half of all Universalist ministers embraced the Spiritualist movement, which sought a scientifically verifiable path to religious truth. A generation later, Unitarians and Universalists were the first to embrace Darwinian science as an ally rather than an enemy of faith.

Other Unitarians and Universalists were reformers. The heart of their religion was building a more just and inclusive society. Universalist shoemaker William Heighton helped launch the labor movement by calling for a political party composed entirely of "Working Men." The brothers Charles and John Murray Spear, both Universalist ministers, befriended prisoners and fought to end the death penalty. Unitarian Lydia Maria Child risked her career as a writer of children's books by demanding immediate abolition of slavery. Ministers Theodore Parker and Thomas Wentworth Higginson were so opposed to slavery that they took up arms to defend fugitives from the South. Adin Ballou, who served both Unitarian and Universalist congregations, was a staunch abolitionist, absolute pacifist, and creator of a utopian community. His writings on nonviolence inspired Leo Tolstoy and Mohandas Gandhi. Universalist and Unitarian women were among the first to be ordained in the United States. Antoinette Brown Blackwell and Olympia Brown combined ministry with agitation for women's suffrage.

Contemporary Unitarian Universalists cherish the memory of the heretics and the reformers. But we would not remember them at all if it weren't for the institution builders. Among the Unitarians, denominational president Henry Whitney Bellows led the way in making space for both Transcendentalists and liberal Christians in a single church. And the Universalists' "grasshopper missionary," Quillen Shinn, hopped to many unlikely corners of America with the message of God's limitless love.

Reaching Out

Unitarians and Universalists never held a monopoly on liberal religion. Many Unitarian Universalists today hold views similar to the eighteenth-century deists and nineteenth-century Freethinkers. Those groups taught a "religion of reason" that only gradually found a home in our tradition. Some of the founders of Unitarianism and Universalism were active Freemasons, and from that tradition they took a commitment to religious tolerance and brotherly love. Unitarians and Universalists have long felt a kinship with the Quaker tradition, with its emphasis on the "inner light" in each person. They also reached out to the Reform movement in Judaism, which stressed ethics over ritual. The Ethical Culture movement founded by a rabbi's son, Felix Adler, abandoned belief in God altogether and worked closely with the radical wing of Unitarianism.

By the turn of the twentieth century, many Congregationalists, Methodists, and other Protestants were preaching a liberal theology similar to that of the Unitarian and Universalist founders. They also proclaimed a "social gospel": true religion was about building a better world. Unitarians and Universalists worked closely with them. At Harvard, Francis Greenwood Peabody introduced sociology into the curriculum for future ministers. More radical activists created organizations that we now think of as secular. Universalist Charles Vail was the national organizer of the Socialist Party. Unitarian Roger Baldwin was the first leader of the American Civil Liberties Union. Unitarians Mary White Ovington and John Haynes Holmes were among the founders of the National Association for the Advancement of Colored People. With Universalist Clarence Skinner, Holmes also launched a network of activist "community churches." Among them was Egbert Ethelred Brown's Harlem Community Church, an important meeting place for African Americans and West Indians and for black socialists and nationalists. Reformers like Holmes, Brown, and Skinner worked closely with a new wave of heretics. Calling themselves "humanists," these heretics put their faith in science and humanity rather than God. Humanist leaders John Dietrich and Curtis Reese both came to Unitarianism from more conservative denominations. Several Unitarians and one Universalist, Clinton Lee Scott, signed the "Humanist Manifesto" that announced their ideas to the world. Meanwhile, other Universalists redefined their tradition to focus on the wisdom of all world faiths.

Once again, institution builders were flexible enough to win the heretics back. As leader of the Massachusetts Universalists, Scott invited a Unitarian humanist named Kenneth Patton to launch an experimental congregation. Its members studied global faiths and contemporary science, treating their church as a workshop for the future. Unitarian president Frederick May Eliot embraced humanists and reached out to Universalists, hoping both groups would help him build a united liberal church.

Unitarianism finally transcended its New England roots through the fellowship movement of the 1940s, 1950s, and 1960s. In communities from Montgomery, Alabama, to Boulder, Colorado, laypeople created congregations without ministerial oversight. Many were closely tied to colleges or research centers. Others provided a church home for radical activists in conservative neighborhoods. Some of the fellowships have grown into thousand-member churches. Others remain small and feisty.

Toward Beloved Community

The new congregations brought their energy into the Unitarian Universalist Association, founded in 1961 as the fruit of Eliot's dream. Many congregations and individuals still proudly call themselves "Unitarian" or "Universalist." Others, especially those who have come to the tradition since consolidation, claim a fully "Unitarian Universalist" identity. Unitarian Universalists played a vital role in the social change movements of the 1960s. Building on the legacy of the NAACP founders, Unitarian minister Homer Jack helped launch the northern sit-in movement in the 1940s, and he guided our tradition's social justice work in the 1960s. Most of the white lawyers who supported Martin Luther King Jr.'s work in Montgomery were members of the local UU fellowship. Unitarian Universalist minister James Reeb and Unitarian Universalist housewife Viola Liuzzo were martyred in Selma, Alabama, where they had joined hundreds of UU ministers in response to the murder of a local African American activist named Jimmie Lee Jackson. Reeb had been a community minister at Boston's Arlington Street Church. Two years later, that same congregation hosted an interfaith liturgy at which opponents of the Vietnam War prayed together as they burned their draft cards.

Not everyone agreed on the best way to foster justice and peace. Many Unitarian Universalists, both white and black, embraced the Black Power movement of the late 1960s. They hoped that economic and cultural empowerment would make beloved community possible. Others feared that Black Power was a betrayal of the integrationist ideal. The General Assembly of 1968 committed $1 million to black-led economic development projects. Debate over that decision consumed the denomination for the next two years. Leaders reduced funding for empowerment, citing a budget crisis. People on both sides left the tradition, hurt and angry. Others stayed or returned, making the struggle against racism and for beloved community one of our defining commitments. The teach-ins on white supremacy conducted in 2017 are just the latest manifestation of an ongoing struggle to uproot racism in our own movement, even as we confront it in the larger society.

Unitarian Universalism has also transformed itself through its encounter with feminism and LGBTQ liberation. When Rev. James Stoll came out as gay in 1969—the first minister in any tradition to do so—he was embraced by other Unitarian Universalists. Our pioneering sexuality education curriculum, About Your Sexuality, was expanded to honor sexual diversity. Similarly, a small contingent of women ministers swelled to a majority within a few decades. The 1977 Women and Religion resolution began a process of removing sexist language and practices from our shared life. As women explored goddess-centered practices, they made neo-paganism an integral part of the spiritual mosaic of our faith. Unitarian Universalist congregations and individuals were at the forefront of the struggle for marriage equality during the first two decades of the twenty-first century.

If the late 1960s were the tumultuous adolescence of Unitarian Universalism, our movement has since settled into a stable maturity. Membership declined in the 1970s but has been steady since then. This is because of our appeal to spiritual seekers, social activists, and interfaith families. In most UU congregations today, Christians, humanists, Jews, Buddhists, pagans, seekers, and others build religious community together. We join in the fight for immigrant rights and for marriage equality, and we help one another find sustaining spiritual practices. Our diverse national leadership guides us on the journey toward beloved community—stumbling frequently, but always striving to learn from the stumbles. As we continue moving forward, we look back with gratitude to the heretics, reformers, and institution builders who came before us.

"May we go forward in purposeful rhythm,
that we may give voice to the melody of our
    imaginations,
the music of our souls,
and all the possibilities of a just world
as we might together create it.
Go in Peace."

MATT MEYER

Spirit of Life

Spir - it of Life, come un - to me.

Sing in my heart all the stir - rings of com -

pas - sion. Blow in the wind, rise in the

sea; move in the hand, giv-ing

life the shape of jus - tice. Roots hold me

close; wings set me free;

Spir - it of Life, come to me, come to me.

Words and music: Carolyn McDade, © 1981 Carolyn McDade

Come, Come, Whoever You Are

Come, come, who - ev - er you

are, wan - der - er, wor - ship - er,

lov - er of leav - ing. Ours is no

car - a - van of _____ de - spair.

Come, yet a - gain come. _____

Words: adapted from Jalaluddin Rumi
Music: Lynn Adair Ungar, © 1989 Lynn Adair Ungar

Gathered Here

Gath - ered here in the mys-t'ry of the hour.

Gath - ered here in one strong bod - y.

Gath - ered here in the strug-gle and the pow'r.

Spir - it, draw near.

Words and music: Philip A. Porter, © 1991 Philip A. Porter

Blue Boat Home

Fluid, legato ♩=140

1. Though be - low me, I feel no
2. Sun my sail__ and moon my
3. I give thanks to the waves up -

mo - tion stand - ing on these
rud - der as I ply the
hold - ing me, hail the great winds

moun - tains and plains. Far a -
star - ry sea, lean - ing
urg - ing me on, greet the

way from the roll - ing o - cean
o - ver the edge in won - der,
in - fi - nite sea be - fore__ me,

still my dry land heart__ can
cast - ing ques - tions in - to the
sing the sky my sail - or's

say: I've been sail - ing
deep. Drift - ing here with my
song: I was born__ up -

Words: Peter Mayer, © 2002 Peter Mayer
Music: Roland Hugh Prichard, adapted by Peter Mayer, © 2002 Peter Mayer

all   my   life   now,   nev - er
ship's   com - pan - ions,   all   we
on   the   fath - oms,   nev - er

har - bor   or   port have   I   known.   The
kin - dred   pil - grim souls,
har - bor   or   port have   I   known.   The

wide   u - ni - verse   is   the   o -
mak - ing   our way   by   the lights
wide   u - ni - verse   is   the   o -

- cean   I   trav - el
of   the   heav - ens
- cean   I   trav - el,

and the earth   is my   blue
in   our beau - ti - ful   blue
and the earth   is my   blue

boat   home.
boat   home.
boat   home.

Meditation on Breathing

Words and music: Sarah Dan Jones, © 2001 Sarah Dan Jones

Resources

UU World, the magazine of the Unitarian Universalist Association (UUA), aims to help its readers build their faith and act on it more effectively in their personal lives, their congregations, their communities, and the world. The print magazine is published quarterly in February, May, August, and November. You can subscribe or read a weekly issue of the free online edition at uuworld.org.

The UUA also publishes a number of pamphlets intended to answer questions you may have about Unitarian Universalism. You can read these online by visiting uua.org/pamphlets.

The following books are available from inSpirit: The UU Book and Gift Shop at uua.org/bookstore.

Ellen Brandenburg, ed., *The Seven Principles in Word and Worship* (Skinner House Books).

John A. Buehrens, *The Universalists and Unitarians in America: A People's History* (Skinner House Books).

Forrest Church and John A. Buehrens, *A Chosen Faith: An Introduction to Unitarian Universalism* (Beacon Press).

Patricia Frevert, ed., *Welcome: A Unitarian Universalist Primer* (Skinner House Books).

Edward A. Frost, *With Purpose and Principle* (Skinner House Books).

Keith Kron and Susan A. Gore, eds., *Coming Out in Faith: Voices of LGBTQ Unitarian Universalists* (Skinner House Books).

Jack Mendelsohn, *Being Liberal in an Illiberal Age: Why I Am a Unitarian Universalist* (Skinner House Books).

Paul Rasor, *Faith Without Certainty: Liberal Theology in the 21st Century* (Skinner House Books).

Meg Riley, ed., *Testimony: The Transformative Power of Unitarian Universalism* (Skinner House Books).

Voices in Unitarian Universalism Series

Wayne Arnason and Sam Trumbore, eds., *Buddhist Voices in Unitarian Universalism* (Skinner House Books).

Kathleen Rolenz, ed., *Christian Voices in Unitarian Universalism* (Skinner House Books).

Kendyl L. R. Gibbons and William R. Murry, eds., *Humanist Voices in Unitarian Universalism* (Skinner House Books).

Leah Hart-Landsberg and Marti Keller, eds., *Jewish Voices in Unitarian Universalism* (Skinner House Books).

Jerrie Kishpaugh Hildebrand and Shirley Ann Ranck, eds., *Pagan and Earth-Centered Voices in Unitarian Universalism* (Skinner House Books).

Songs and Readings

Lifting Our Voices: Readings in the Living Tradition (Unitarian Universalist Association).

Singing the Journey (Unitarian Universalist Association).

Singing the Living Tradition (Unitarian Universalist Association).

Kathleen Rolenz, ed., *Sources of Our Faith* (Skinner House Books).

For Children

Pam Baxter, *A Cup of Light* (Skinner House Books).

Jennifer Dant, *Everybody Is Important: A Kids' Guide to Our Seven Principles* (Skinner House Books).

Jennifer Dant, *Unitarian Universalism Is a Really Long Name* (Skinner House Books).

Patricia Frevert, ed., *Sunday and Every Day: My Little Book of Unitarian Universalism* (Skinner House Books).